Becoming
a Woman
of Interior
Elegance

An Inspirational Book for Women

LaTan Roland Murphy

CONTENTS

Acknowledgements   v
Introduction
Elegance   vii

1.   Inelegant Moments   1
2.   Casting out Demons   7
3.   The Power of the Pause   13
4.   From Eve's Garden into Our World   19
5.   Fading Beauty   27
6.   Betsy   33
7.   Joy   41
8.   When Joy Leaves Town   47
9.   Listen…He Is Speaking   53
10. My Interior Decorating Friend   61
11. Pansy Moments   67
12. Playing Dress Up   73
13. Removing the Masks   77
14. She Stooped to Conquer   85
15. Women of Interior Elegance   91
16. Her Name is Depression   95
17. Stand Still. Don't Run   101
18. The Giving Trees   107
19. The Fence   117
20. The Other Man   123
21. Mustard Seed Faith   129
22. Knowing Who You Are In Christ   137
23. From Smiles to Scowls   143
24. From Humiliation to Humor   149
25. Beyond the Walls   155
26. Christian   161
27. Mother of the Year   167
28. True Inner Beauty   173
29. Be a Friend, Have a Friend   177
30. Setting the Mood of Your Home   185
31. Elegant Warrior   191
32. Miracle at the Gate   195

33. The Focal Point   201
34. God is Good   207
35. Defending Others   211
36. Good Enough   215
37. Bring Back Those Dying Dreams   223
38. A Beautiful Plan Gone Wrong   229
39. You Did Good, Baby   235
40. A Window with a View   239
41. Abundant Life   247
42. Hector   253
43. I Watched You   259
44. My Grandmother's Chair   265
45. What's Your Anaconda?   271
46. Sweet Tea with Lemons   277
47. Puppy Chow   283
48. Simmering Potpourri   289

Following the Path   295

Acknowledgements

I have been blessed to have strong, elegant women in my life. Each bravely walked through trials that would have caused most people to crumble. Through the years, I have been amazed and inspired by the refining, elegant image of Christ reflected in their lives. These tenacious women taught me the powerful gift of laughter when facing some of life's most embarrassing moments—proving the joy of the Lord is good medicine for the soul.

Words cannot express how grateful I am to my wonderful, late mother-in-law, Mrs. Betty Murphy, who was determined to see my name published on a book. She courageously suffered a long battle with cancer, all the while inspiring many through faith and good deeds. Thank you Mom Murphy, for the gift of your son. He is a wonderful husband because of your parenting, and I am reaping the harvest of your labor. You are loved and greatly missed!

Thanks to my mother, Mrs. Nadine Roland. You are a gift to my generation. You laughed at me when I told you I wanted to be just like you when I grow up. I meant it. Your courageous heart inspires me. You dreamt of writing a book of your own—little did you know you were writing a biography of Jesus. You wrote it across the pages of my heart and taught Christ's character in the way you responded to circumstances in your own life. You have been through just about everything a person could go through in this life. The joy of the Lord has proven to be your source of strength and I will take that forward.

I could not have written this book without the loving support of my wonderful husband, Joe. Thank you for always loving me, even on my most inelegant days. Thank you for seeing beyond my human frailty, and for pointing out the elegant beauty of Christ on the interior of my heart when I could not see it. I praise the Lord for giving me the honor of being your wife.

Editor: Carolyn Murphy—Thank you for being such a wonderful daughter to us. God truly blessed our son with an angel. We love you deeply!

BECOME
His Will

DO
His Will

And we, who with unveiled faces all reflect the Lord's glory, are being transformed into his likeness with ever-increasing glory, which comes from the Lord, who is the Spirit.

2 Corinthians 3:18 (NIV)

Love the Lord your God with all your heart and with all your soul and with all your strength.

Deuteronomy 6:5 (NIV)

Introduction

ELEGANCE

Time fades beauty. But time cannot fade a beautiful, elegant spirit. For true beauty comes from within.

Have you ever seen a gorgeous woman with a really bad attitude about life? Because of her poor behavior, her beauty is significantly diminished. Some of the most beautiful women we will ever encounter are women who know who they are in Christ.

A woman of interior elegance has confidence, there is a beautiful light that radiate inside of her, drawing people to her in wonder of what makes her so unique and special. Her life is marked by peaceful living. When she looks in the mirror, she is content because she knows who she is in the eyes of her maker.

She avoids pointless efforts to control or change others, and instead focuses on changing herself for the better. She is settled and content. Manipulating situations or people to suit her own personal agenda is never on her radar. Wisely, she leaves the judging of others up to God.

The elegant woman of God is fully aware of her frailty in light of God's power. She leans hard into his strength when hers fails.

When circumstances threaten to rob her joy or snatch her purpose, when life seems far from picture perfect, the elegant woman leans harder into her faith. Even when the pressures of life are most intense, she willingly allows Christ to be exemplified. His elegant spirit turns bitter situations into better ones.

The elegant woman of God takes good care of her physical appearance because her body is the temple of God. He lives in her, loves through her, and helps her to live a powerful and productive life.

Let's take the first step together—step out onto the path leading to interior elegance as defined by God's standards.

⚘

THE ELEGANT WOMAN OF GOD IS MOST CONCERNED WITH HER INTERNAL BEAUTY.

Charm is deceptive, and beauty is fleeting; but a woman who fears the Lord is to be praised. Proverbs 31:30 (NIV)

CHAPTER ONE

INELEGANT MOMENTS

The sermon was one of the most spiritually moving sermons I had heard in a long time. As I listened intently to the pastor's tender words, I became emotional. My husband and I, unfortunately, had decided to sit three rows from the front of the church. I reached into my purse for a tissue to wipe my tears; my eyes never leaving the pastor as he continued to preach. As I raised the tissue to my nose, I felt something sticky and heard the crinkle of paper. Just before blowing my nose, I pulled back. To my shock and dismay, I was about to blow my nose, not on a tissue, but a panty liner!

Oh yes, third row from the front of the church. Not exactly an *elegant moment*, would you say? As *Murphy's Law* would have it, (I guess I can say that literally since we are the Murphy family) my husband looked over towards me at the very moment in which the panty liner made contact with my nose. He rolled his eyes and mumbled, "Oh my word."

Needless to say, the pew and our bodies were shaking to the same rhythm, as we laughed hysterically. Neither of us heard another word of the sermon, and I am pretty sure none of the good folk sitting near us did either!

On another occasion, my husband surprised me with tickets to see *The Phantom of the Opera*. I was excited beyond words and desperately wanted to make it an extra-special night for him. After slipping into, or perhaps I should say 'squeezing' into my black sheath dress, I felt a bit like a giant strawberry dipped in chocolate, and was totally distressed. The elastic waistband on my panty hose was too tight. The sheath dress showed no mercy and seemed determined to display every hump and bump; there was no way to hide my love for chocolate chip cookie dough. The straight lines of my dress screamed of my indulgence. As I stood in front of the mirror, the fantasy of how beautiful I would look for my husband suddenly melted away into the elastic waistband of my panty hose.

Determined not to be discouraged—regardless of the fact that I resembled a balloon at the county fair, twisted into animal shapes by the clowns–I picked up the phone and called a girlfriend for help. She updated me on the latest fashion invention: thigh-high hose. She promised, "You won't even need to wear the garter. They stay up great on your legs!" *Perfect!*

I went immediately to the store to purchase a lifesaving pair of thigh-highs. Hours later, dressed and ready to go to the ball, (Oops! the Opera) – I felt like a million dollars in my sheath dress. What fun it would be to surprise my husband later in the evening with my miraculous thigh-highs. I couldn't wait to see the shock on his face—especially given the fact that I usually sleep in ugly, flannel, cow-jump-over-the-moon pajamas.

When we arrived, most of the parking lots were already full because I had taken so long to get dressed. We were late. The few parking spots left were in an area I will refer to as the *South Pole*. My husband opened the door of our *golden carriage*. Ha! I meant to say, he opened the door of our Buick LeSabre, and off we went across the crowded parking lot.

We were about half way across the parking lot when I felt something strange happening to my left thigh-high: it was rolling down my leg. My thoughts were racing, thinking of how my friend was going to get the '*what-for.*' She had promised they wouldn't slip down! Now the real problem was that my beautiful sheath dress had a slit up the center front, stopping just above my knees. Each step I took, the thigh-high went further and further down my leg. There was no hiding it, for it had rolled so far down it was now in full view of God and man.

This wasn't the way I had envisioned surprising my husband. Oh, he was surprised alright. "What's that?" he asked, as he pointed down toward my knee. The roll of nylon had stopped rolling down, only because I had stopped moving.

"Find a bathroom, quick." I responded.

As we began to climb the multitude of stairs leading up to the auditorium, I realized the car would have been a much better place to have gone, because by now my thigh-high was below my knee. Each step I took, the slit in my dress announced my demise to the massive crowd looking on; my roll of nylon screamed out to them! I was mortified–a toxic, emotional mix of disbelief and total horror.

I'll go upstairs to find a bathroom, I thought, racing toward the elevator. Looking down toward my legs, I entered the open elevator doors. While still surveying my problem, I turned completely back toward the doors. After realizing I was alone, proceeded to remove my high heel shoes. I moved quickly—knowing I had to complete the task before the elevator arrived on the next floor. Pulling my dress up higher, I happily rid myself of my run-away thigh-highs. *What an ingenious idea,* I thought, pulling my dress back down. After smoothing and straightening my tightly fitted dress, I slipped my shoes back onto my bare feet, drew in a deep cleansing breath, and exhaled a sigh of relief. With a sense of accomplishment, I pushed the elevator button to return to the lower level and smiled with pleasure that I'd avoided the long bathroom lines. I began looking around inside the elevator. *So much for surprising him,* I thought, while scanning the walls. I glanced at the backside of the elevator, and it was there that I froze into place. The entire back wall of the elevator was *glass!* The faces peering back at me from the other side confirmed that this was reality–what an unwanted surprise they had received. I was sure most of those looking on would need counseling for the rest of their lives because of the trauma they had experienced. When the elevator door opened, I sheepishly stepped out, trying to avoid the stares. My face was burning with embarrassment. *"Where are your hose,"* my husband asked, as I approached him. *"I'll tell you later,"* I replied.

Friends, when something like this happens, you have two choices: you can die of embarrassment, or you can die laughing! I chose what any elegant woman would do, I laughed at myself and let my husband die of embarrassment.

Laughter really is a gift. I hope you are able to laugh at yourself, sweet friends. Laughter is good medicine. I am convinced that laughter works against gravity and keeps us looking young, because it forces all of our wrinkles to turn upward. Don't ever be too proud to share an embarrassing moment with someone. Let go of the pride that hinders you. In doing so, you will free others to be real. Ask the Lord to fill you with the confidence that comes from knowing who you are in Christ. Then you will be able to share your *inelegant moments* with someone else who just might need a *face-lift.* You may have the opportunity to brighten another person's day with a little good, old-fashioned laughter—at your own expense, of course.

THE ELEGANT WOMAN OF GOD FINDS HUMOR IN EVERY UNPLEASANT EVENT.

May the God of hope fill you with all joy and peace as you trust in him, so that you may overflow with hope by the power of the Holy Spirit.
Romans 15:13 (NIV)

ELEGANT REFLECTIONS

What is the most embarrassing moment you have ever experienced?

_____
_____
_____
_____

How does knowing who you are in Christ help when you are faced with humiliating circumstances?

_____
_____
_____
_____

Read Romans 15:13.

How do hope and joy enrich our lives?

_____
_____
_____
_____

Write your heart-felt prayer here:

_____
_____
_____
_____

What hinders us from sharing the embarrassing moments we face in life?

_____
_____
_____
_____

Note: It took many years for me to find the courage to share these embarrassing moments. Pride was a huge factor in my reluctance to share. I finally realized by sharing, I was not only giving the gift of joy and laughter to others, I was also freeing myself from the grip of a pride-driven spirit.

Have you ever dealt with pride? How has pride affected your life?

_____

_____

_____

_____

Prayer: "Father, I pray you will fill me with joy, hope and peace each day. Help me live in freedom, knowing you love me no matter what. I surrender my pride today. Help me to be real and transparent before you and others." Amen.

CHAPTER TWO

CASTING OUT DEMONS

I was so frustrated. I could not think of anything to say that would make my husband understand where I was coming from. He was wrong, plain and simple. We women think we are always right, you know. After all, aren't we an infinite wealth of wisdom?

We had been married only a few years and were still working out a few kinks in our communication skills. Although I could count on one hand how many arguments we had had up to this point, this was without a doubt the granddaddy of them all. We were both emotionally out of control, and could not even listen to what the other was trying to convey. Today, if you were to ask either of us what the argument was about, neither of us could tell you.

While my husband was in mid-sentence, I remembered listening, earlier in the week, to *Focus on the Family*-Dr. James Dobson's family broadcast. My husband's voice began to sound much like Charlie Brown's teacher as I drifted off in thought. Pride began to fill every empty recess of my angry heart, as I devised a plan to confront my husband the same way Dr. Dobson's guest speaker had confronted her daughter when having trouble communicating.

On the broadcast, the guest speaker had shared candidly about her daughter's anger issues and her inability to communicate with her. Each time the mother approached her daughter, anger escaladed out of control. When she finally recognized the spirit within the room as an evil force trying to break down communication between the two of them, she took action. She pointed her finger at the girl, and with a voice of authority said, "I rebuke you in the name of Jesus Christ." Immediately, the spirit lifted from the room and the communication barrier was broken.

As I stood there in front of the kind, gentle man I had married, wondering to myself how in the world I could break through to him in his moment of uncontrolled anger and stubbornness, an ingenious idea presented itself to me. I would do just as the mother on James Dobson's program had done. I must admit I was excited. I felt I had true *spiritual* ammunition he simply could not argue with.

I stood there with my arms folded, thinking, *"Boy, are you in for the surprise of your life."*

With smoke coming from my ears and my right index finger aiming directly toward his face, I spoke with authority in my voice and with a self-righteous tone, *"I rebuke you in the name of Jesus Christ."*

I knew from the expression on his face that I had made a terrible mistake. Girls, it was not an elegant moment.

Suddenly, without warning, this gentle man who had rarely even raised his voice at me lifted his large hand to my still pointed finger. With fire blazing from his green eyes, a fire resembling the embers of a wild forest fire, he said in a voice that let me know he meant business, *"You want to see demons. I'll show you some demons."*

You can imagine my shock and dismay. I wanted to shout, *"Who are you and what **have you done with my husband?"***

I learned some very important lessons that day. I have listed a few of them below:

- I am not the boss and would not be wearing the pants in our family.
- It is not my responsibility to cast demons out of other people, especially my husband.
- There will always be differences of opinions. I am not always right; others are not always wrong.
- I need to pray for wisdom before I open my mouth to speak.
- I need to ask the Lord if my opinion will change the situation for good. If not, I should keep my opinion to myself.
- The most powerful conversation I will ever have is through prayer.
- Instead of taking control, I must practice taking my concerns and frustrations to Christ.
- I must trust Christ's power to change others. He does a much better job.

So, the next time you are tempted to cast the demons out of those with whom you just can't see eye-to-eye, take a deep breath and pray for wisdom—*before pointing a finger!*

THE ELEGANT WOMAN OF GOD IS A GREAT LISTENER. SHE LISTENS MORE THAN SHE TALKS, AND IS SLOW TO BECOME ANGRY.

Everyone should be quick to listen, slow to speak and slow to become angry.
James 1:19 (NIV)

ELEGANT REFLECTIONS

Read James 1:19 (NIV): *Everyone should be quick to listen, slow to speak and slow to become angry.*

Are you quick to listen?

_____

_____

_____

_____

Are you slow to speak?

_____

_____

_____

_____

Are you slow to become angry?

_____

_____

_____

_____

Confess to the Lord which of these you need to work toward in order to become a woman of interior elegance?

_____

_____

_____

_____

Have you ever tried to 'cast out demons' in others, instead of sweeping around your own front door?

_____

_____

_____

_____

Note: Do everything you can to honor others—even when you don't agree with them, or see eye-to-eye. Isn't it a relief to know you don't need to be the Holy Spirit in the lives of others?

Prayer: "Father, help me to be quick to listen, slow to speak and slow to become angry. I want to be transformed by your holy power. Teach me your ways and help me to live according to your perfect will." Amen.

CHAPTER THREE

THE POWER OF THE PAUSE

I said something I should not have said. I wished to take it back, but it was too late. Oh, my friend, if you only knew how many times I have done this. After the fact, I always end up with thoughts of regret, feelings of insecurity, and an overwhelming sense of guilt. Can you identify?

One important thing I am learning on my journey to become a woman of interior elegance is: *the power of the pause.* Not an easy thing to do but the times I have disciplined my tongue to wait a minute before rushing in to speak, I have been thankful later. By no means have I mastered pausing. Let me not mislead you into believing that I am a perfectly eloquent lady of God, although that is exactly what I long to be. I am still learning, growing, and **becoming** a woman of interior elegance—a work in progress!

There are few disciplines in the Christian life that will refine your character as much as pausing will, but pausing requires practice. In order to become a woman of interior elegance, our *spirit-girl* must demand that our *flesh-girl* learn to pause. This involves waiting a minute before we speak, maybe even two. In certain situations, it is best to wait days before responding or speaking out. This is really hard for those of us who feel we are an infinite wealth of wisdom. Withholding our thoughts on a matter we are passionate about is brutally difficult for those of us who suffer from a condition I have personally named— ***Impulsive Impatient Disorder: I.I.D***. Pausing long enough to evaluate the over-all impact our words will have on others is key to becoming a woman of interior elegance.

Like a gold ring in a pig's snout is a beautiful woman who shows no discretion.
Proverbs 11:22 (NIV).

Many times a pause has kept me from saying something stupid. Other times, pausing has literally rescued me from participating in conversations that borderline on gossip. I have not always listened to that still, small voice but have rushed in to speak my case as if the world itself depended on my opinion alone. Then had a rude awakening upon realizing my opinions were meaningless in the scheme of things.

Many stories have been repeated without giving careful consideration to the source from which it came. We have lost our search for real truth among the maze of information that makes us feel important in retelling it. We long to seem important to others. That longing often gets us into big trouble. There is power in pausing, for in the pause, there is no room for regret. There is, however, time: to collect one's thoughts, to think about what kind of effect this information could have on another person, and to evaluate the level of explosiveness that could occur because of the information being passed along to the wrong person.

As women, we often struggle with the idea of pausing before we speak. We have an agenda and feel it our personal duty to see it through to the end. This is more of a temptation for some than for others. I encourage you to be aware of tendencies to get caught up in conversations that aren't fruitful or beneficial.

As I said before, the most difficult thing about pausing is it involves waiting. Waiting is the farthest thing on our minds when we feel passionate about something. We feel we must speak our mind or we might die. Oh, what a tangled web we weave when *we with a cause, refuse to pause.*

It is much easier said than done. The previous chapter bears witness to the fact that I struggle with the pause as well. At times, out of my mouth have come such inelegant things for which I feel so very ashamed. (Like the time I tried to cast demons out of my husband!) When I have felt justified in my cause, I have found it difficult to pause. *"I must be right,"* or *"Things must be my way."* These thoughts have played into my subconscious piety.

Are you a person to be trusted? When people hear you talk ill of someone else, how could they not question what you would say of them when they are not in your presence? A woman of interior elegance will desire to think elegant thoughts so she can speak elegant words. Elegant thoughts refine her responses. Elegant words spoken have power to edify and build up. This requires discipline. This requires holding ourselves accountable to a higher standard: being a bit harder on ourselves than we are on others.

Do you want others to know without a shadow of a doubt that when you speak, you are speaking truth? Do you want them to know you stick to the facts when repeating stories? I believe you do. Let's strive together toward the goal of elegance. I want there to be a deep level of confidentiality that goes far beyond explanation. When we are found in difficult situations, whether temptation to repeat information that is not ours to share, or some painful confrontation, let's determine in our hearts not to be found standing in the shadows of private shame and guilt, but in His light—pausing elegantly!

THE ELEGANT WOMAN OF GOD IS WISE AND DISCERNING.

She opens her mouth with skillful and godly wisdom, and in her tongue is the law of kindness giving counsel and instruction.
Proverbs 31:26 (NIV)

ELEGANT REFLECTIONS

Reread Proverbs 11:22 (NIV): *Like a gold ring in a pig's snout is a beautiful woman who shows no discretion.*

Describe how indiscretion changes your view of someone.

_____

_____

_____

_____

_____

_____

Do you feel you use discretion? Are you confidential?

_____

_____

_____

_____

_____

_____

Do you trust people who gossip about others? If not, do you still listen to the gossip? How could this choice affect others' trust in you?

_____

_____

_____

_____

_____

_____

What is God trying to tell us in the following scripture verse?

Like a gold ring in a pig's snout is a beautiful woman who use no discretion?
Proverbs 11:22 (NIV)

_____

_____

_____

_____

_____

_____

_____

Prayer: "Father, I want to be a woman who can be trusted. Help me use discretion when necessary. Make the words of my mouth fruitful and wise." Amen.

CHAPTER FOUR

FROM EVE'S GARDEN INTO OUR WORLD

E ve was the first woman created by God. She too, experienced inelegant days when her out-of-control thought-life resulted in sinful behavior.

Friend, we all have experienced wanting something we know we should not pursue. We say, "I've just got to have it!" The thing Eve just *had to have*—the forbidden fruit—was the one thing God had spoken against.

Eve was a lady who had it made and didn't even know it! Think of it, she was the only woman in a perfect world, the Garden of Eden. She didn't have to wear makeup, push-up bras, or thigh-highs. There were no other women with whom to compete.

Adam wasn't off somewhere on a business trip, tempted to look at inappropriate movies. He wasn't off in the corner of the garden, reclining on a rock. He wasn't hanging from a tree in a hammock watching the sports channel, remote control in hand. He wasn't swinging from vine to vine, stopping for a short pleasure break in the highest and most scenic tree in Eden in order to get the best view of the female race swinging nearby.

No, Eve didn't have any concerns such as: "I don't fill my fig leaf out right," or "there's so much extra hanging over that I can't see my fig leaf." She didn't have to spend hours shopping at *Fig Leaf Fashions* to find just the right leaf to wear. No, instead, she was naked and unashamed before her lover, beautiful in his eyes and unlike any other creature on earth.

Eve was perfect, but somewhere along her journey, her world did not seem so perfect. She could no longer see the blessings for the bushes. Just think about the day the snake came into the garden. She must have had inelegant feelings long before he slithered into Eden on the Snake Train. She must have bought his ticket, paid the train fare, and waited there to give him a welcome party.

Do you find yourself unaware of your blessings? I sure do! By failing to count our blessings, we set the stage for Satan to play the role of leading man in our lives. Instead of God's power transforming our thoughts, Satan gets busy taking us emotionally captive. If not on-guard against his evil schemes, we will slowly become dissatisfied with our lives.

What led to Eve's initiating the fall of man? What was so enticing about the fruit of that particular tree? I've given this some thought and would like to share some of my ideas with you.

I wonder if the tree of forbidden fruit had every kind of fruit opposite the fruit of God's spirit. The fruits of the spirit are: love, joy, peace, longsuffering, gentleness, goodness, faithfulness, meekness, and self-control. Discontentment entered into Eve's heart. Perhaps that was when her inelegant emotion gave way to sin.

Maybe it started with ungratefulness for all she had in her perfect garden home. Maybe she began to question if her home was good enough or if there could be more to life outside the grove. Maybe she began to criticize her husband, her love for him becoming clouded with frustration to control or fix him.

The peace-filled paradise God had given her was no longer enough. Discontentment had its way as she allowed Satan's voice to over-ride God's voice. She became restless. Perhaps she could no longer discern how blessed she was. Her joy melted into an ocean of depression: her once patience-now impatience; her kind heart-now bitter and envious, wanting more and more of the wrong things; her once unwavering faith, now wavering. The fruit of God's spirit could no longer satisfy Eve.

Eve signed an invisible contract with Satan that day that would put all women in bondage for generations to come. She traded the fruit of God's spirit for the fruit of Satan's spirit. I wonder if she ate first with slow, reluctant nibbles as she fought against truth. As her appetite for sin increased, did she eat with full-force?

Reality slammed into her guilt-ridden soul. How could she have been so blind? Perhaps her heart cried out, "Oh, if only I had known how blessed I truly was!"

Shame settled in but it was too late. She looked back over her shoulder and saw the beauty of her home from a distance— *The Garden of Eden*, as if for the first time. We somehow see things for what they truly are when we have lost everything. She must have been tormented by her thoughts: *"How did I wander so far from the place where God's spirit flowed so freely?"* We must be slow to throw stones at her for if we could look into her eyes, we would see a part of ourselves.

Eve had failed and now she was banished out of Eden with Satan. She had to start over outside the beauty and blessings of the garden. She did, with God's help. It was not an easy journey, for she had given a part of herself to the master of destruction and had to reclaim the prize to reach her goal. It was a fight to the end, for Eden was back there somewhere in her heart and mind. Eden represented a world of beauty and blessing she had taken for granted. She would live in constant regret.

We have much to learn from Eve's choices. We are not hopeless in our struggle. God will help us start fresh today. He will dominate the inelegant ugliness that discontentment causes.

Let us learn from Eve's temptation. We must remember the tree standing on the edge of Eden, forbidden fruit spilling from its branches. Our hearts must travel back to the center of Eden where a much stronger tree stands with His branches stretched out in the form of a cross, standing strong and true forever. Reaching even now from Eden into our world, the perfect fruit of His empowering spirit is ready for harvest. The tree of life overflows in abundance with the fruit of His spirit. We must eat from it. Let us eat with full-force. May our hearts be refined and cleansed. Our souls will be renewed, as we willingly allow God's full-authority to dominate our lives. It was at the forbidden tree we lost everything, but, at the tree in the form of a cross, we are given new life.

Beware! Because of sin, our homes will be Satan's prey. His number one goal is to destroy our marriages and our children. He thrives on discontentment. Choose contentment today, my friend. Be thankful. Rejoice. God is fighting for you. He will fight to the end. Christ already won every battle you and I will ever face.

Stand strong, elegant women of God. Continue the journey without looking back, without regret. Look forward to the bright future the Creator has planned for you. Press on toward the prize. As Christ's power cleanses and refines us into His elegant image, we will jump up and down in celebrated fashion as we kick Satan out of our garden home, forever. Only then, will we slowly begin to feel elegant again.

Run to the tree bearing every good fruit. Feast on the fruit of His spirit and live!

THE ELEGANT WOMAN OF GOD REALIZES WHAT SHE HAS TO BE THANKFUL FOR, EMBRACES IT AND REALLY LIVES!

Give thanks in all circumstances, for this is God's will for you in Christ Jesus.
Thessalonians 5:18 (NIV)

ELEGANT REFLECTIONS

Have you ever experienced discontentment?

_____

_____

_____

_____

How does an attitude of gratitude help in times of discontentment?

_____

_____

_____

_____

Write three things you are grateful for in the space below:

_____

_____

_____

_____

Reread the following: Thessalonians 5:18 (NIV): *"Give thanks in all circumstances, for this is God's will for you in Christ Jesus."*

Think about the circumstances you are facing. How difficult is it for you to give thanks?

_____

_____

_____

_____

What happens when we waste our time looking back to the past while living in regret?

_____

_____

_____

_____

Note: We often find ourselves curious. We can have sympathy for Eve because we tend to be drawn to the things we know are off-limits. Giving in to temptation is not in our best interest, so why do we? Many times, we repeat the same thing (sin) over and over, even though we know we will face sad results, laced with guilt. Confess your sin to the Lord in the space below. Ask for strength to stop compromising. Be done with your old patterns and start fresh today.

_____

_____

_____

_____

Prayer: "Father, Give me a spirit of contentment. Help me to thank you even when I am afraid or unsure of my future. I want to be in the center of your will— thankful in all circumstances." Amen.

Chapter Five

FADING BEAUTY

I am standing in front of the mirror. The person I see looking back at me looks familiar. She has a striking resemblance to someone I know. But this woman could not be me.

She has small lines trellising across her under eye area, drawing attention to the puffiness there. *"You could pack groceries in those bags, girl!"* The skin is beginning to sag under her chin, moving down toward her neck. If sags could be people, they'd be triplets! I now understand what a turtleneck is!

A few more grey hairs remind me that the girl I used to be is forever fading into a new person. A person I barely recognize. No, this could not be the confident young woman that once looked back at me: eyes vibrant, skin tight, hair shiny and alive.

I look down at my legs. Broken veins now create a road map to some place unimaginable. Where did that cellulite come from? It's as if what once was smooth as a prairie now sings a new song entitled: *The Hills Are*

Alive. I realize I will never be the same. I am a little sad about it, although I am learning to be comfortable in the new version of me.

I glanced into a mirror at the mall one day and thought I was some-one else, a stranger perhaps, but with features so strikingly familiar to my own. There I stood, face-to-face with her. Reality was not kind. I had never noticed the change. It just sort of crept up on me–happened al-most overnight. I even bought the night cream!

I am no longer thin. No, my stomach is much like a hide-away sofa that is rolled and tucked away daily as I dress myself. Everything that was once up north is slowly but surely, falling down south. I finally fig-ured out why folks used to say, "When you get older you'll settle down." I didn't know it had anything to do with my physical self.

Do you find yourself groaning and moaning more frequently about aches and pains? I do! Ben-Gay and I have a very close and intimate relationship.

I know, I know, what I need is an exercise regimen. It seems I am doing more hand-to-mouth aerobics than any other kind of exercise these days. I even made up a little exercise chant to help me keep rhythm. It goes like this, *"Up and down and open that mouth and chew it well, now get another bite. Now lift that fork and down we go, now take a drink of soda before we choke!"*

I remember listening to my mother and her friend as they discussed their latest and greatest dieting strategies. They were a little disillusioned by the aging process. I must have been about seventeen years old–so full of wisdom, you know. After listening intently without even a morsel of sympathy, I proceeded to give them a sermon on how they should enjoy the process of aging and grow old graciously and gracefully. Well, now that I am in the aging dilemma, I understand. And somewhere in the distance I can hear voices singing, "The old gray mule just ain't what she used to be."

I am placing much less emphasis on my outward appearance these days. It's a good thing because there is much less there. I am getting a new attitude, and a new focus.

We live in a society whose main focus seems to be on the outward appearance. Most commercials and magazine covers try to dictate what we should look like and how we should dress. They all have a quick fix for weight loss and a new idea, monthly, as to how we can win friends and feel accepted by all. If we put stock in these things, we will find our self-worth diminishing into a puddle of disappointment and insecurities.

I do want to grow old gracefully, to be focused on Christ and not on self-pity. I want to be refined by the Spirit of God in order to draw attention to His glory instead of my own.

Sweet friend, let's agree to allow Christ to change us from the inside out. Stand strong. Be determined. Be set-apart. Become a woman of interior elegance and be the right example. Masses of young women are tormented by images the world defines as true beauty. Let's choose to be more concerned about what Christ says about us and less concerned about what the world says we should be. Let's listen for the voice of truth instead of the voice of the destroyer.

We are getting better each day because we are being transformed from the inside out. Seek wisdom instead of chasing after an empty self-image. Take it from me—you will only exhaust yourself emotionally. Determine to be better because of the aging process, instead of becoming bitter. Wrinkles aren't really wrinkles at all—they are character lines that will hopefully line-up with the character of God, someday.

True beauty starts on the interior of one's heart and over-flows as blessings for others. Let's agree to fill our mind with the word of God each day. His word will transform us from the inside out. Read it daily, be amazed. The changing power will flow into every empty recess of our insecure hearts—creating elegant women of God—equipped and ready to change the world.

THE ELEGANT WOMAN OF GOD CELEBRATES HER INNER BEAUTY.

She clothes herself in strength and dignity; she can laugh at the days to come.
Proverbs 31:25 (NIV)

ELEGANT REFLECTIONS

Reread and reflect on Proverbs 31:25. What do you think it means to be clothed in strength and dignity?

_____
_____
_____
_____

What does it mean to be able to laugh at the days to come?

_____
_____
_____
_____

Where do you find your confidence? Is it found in the Lord, or in external things?

_____
_____
_____
_____

How have you changed internally as you have aged? Has the change been positive or negative?

_____
_____
_____
_____

Write in the space below an honest account of the lies your mirror reflects. How have these lies affected your self-esteem?

_____
_____
_____
_____

Do you focus more on your outer beauty or your inner beauty?

_____

_____

_____

_____

Note: Listen for the voice of the Lord as He whispers truth going forward.

Prayer: "Father, I am not the same girl I once was. Life has taken a toll on me. Renew me. Encourage my heart today. Teach me to laugh at the days to come. I know my hope is in you. You are my source of strength and confidence. Help me reflect your glory in every season of life. Remind me that my beauty is found in you alone."

Amen.

CHAPTER SIX

BETSY

With tears streaming down her face, she sat holding the broken wheel in her hands. Her wheel-chair was tilted so far to the left—a dead giveaway that she needed help. My son and I were lost in an area of town that no one, other than those who lived there, would choose to go into alone. Just across the street from the lady, a group of young people watched. No one was willing to come to her rescue. I turned to my son as we waited for the light to change from red to green and said, "Oh Kyle, we have to help!"

We said a quick prayer for protection. I parked the car. Walking quickly towards her, I saw the stream of tears more closely now. She was dirty and barefoot on this much too cool October morning. I looked down to assess the situation fully. The wheel on her chair to my left was torn completely in half. She had been stranded for quite some time. Her tears had created a path down her unwashed face. She was in terrible need of a bath.

"Honey, what is your name?" I asked, leaning down to touch her shoulder.

"Betsy."

"What can we do to help you?"

"I need to get to the bus stop so I can go to the bank to get some money. Then I can go to the medical supply office to get this old tire replaced."

I asked her if she knew the way to the medical supply office. Then, I told her I would be happy to take her there. She didn't know how to direct me because she was so used to riding the bus and had not paid attention to directions.

"What can we do for you, then?"

"I just need some tape. A police officer taped it together two days ago and it worked beautifully."

I began to wave my arms in the air in an attempt to stop some pass-ersby who might have tape in their possession. A telephone service truck came by. *Surely he would have some really sturdy tape.* He would not stop. A construction worker came by in a large truck. *Maybe he will help us,* I thought while waving my arms in the air. But he did not stop.

I turned to my son and said, "Kyle, please pray that someone who has tape will stop and help us."

A few minutes later, an elderly couple stopped at the light. I walked over to the car with a friendly wave, mouthing to them, "Please help us."

He rolled his window down just a bit. I am sure they too, felt unsafe in this section of town.

"Sir, do you have any tape? This woman needs help: the wheel of her chair is torn in half."

He interrupted my pitiful plea as he handed a roll of *scotch tape* out the slightly opened car window. I looked down, thinking to myself, *"This will take an absolute miracle."*

The look in my son's eyes as I approached him told me he was thinking the very same thing. He validated my thoughts when he said, "Mom, there is no way that scotch tape is going to work."

Our eyes met intently. "I know, Kyle, but please pray for a miracle."

Behind my sunglasses, my own tears began to stream down—much the same as the old woman's.

"Dear Jesus, we pray for a miracle for this woman today. Please let this scotch tape work."

Kyle lifted her chair to the right as I put the mended tire back on the rim. We stood back in absolute amazement as the old woman pushed the start button on the wheelchair arm. She sat straight and tall. Our hearts melted as we watched her proudly move down the street toward the bus stop. I said to my son, "She is so happy, you would think she is driving a red Lamborghini." We were frozen in place watching, amazed at the true miracle we had witnessed, first-hand. The Lord spoke to my heart that morning in such a real way. I shared with my son later.

"Kyle, sometimes we feel like we have nothing to give. Sometimes in life, we think the Lord could not see anything worthy or useful. But in reality, all He wants from us is our scotch tape. The very thing Satan says is most useless, God says: "I can use that! Give all that you have to me and watch me do amazing things!"

I will never forget that day as long as I live. It was one of those rare moments when I was attentive to a need and was so blessed from obedience. My son and I will forever keep the memory of an old woman named Betsy and the truth of what God can do with a roll of scotch tape, tucked deep within the pockets of our hearts.

THE ELEGANT WOMAN OF GOD IS NEVER TOO BUSY TO HELP THOSE IN NEED.

A kindhearted woman gains respect, but ruthless men gain only wealth.
Proverbs 11:16 (NIV)

ELEGANT REFLECTIONS

What does your schedule look like each day?

_____
_____
_____
_____

Does your schedule include helping someone in need?

_____
_____
_____
_____

When we choose to be others-minded, how does it help our mind?

_____
_____
_____
_____

Reread Proverbs 11:16. Why do you think a kind-hearted woman gains respect from others?

_____
_____
_____
_____

Think about the women in your life who have been women of interior elegance. What characteristic did you most admire and desire to model your life after?

_____
_____
_____
_____

How does a ruthless man gain wealth?

_____

_____

_____

_____

List a few ways you can help someone in need each day.

_____

_____

_____

_____

We were lost in an area we had not planned to go, but God used our being lost in order to glorify Him through service to others. Was there ever a time when you were lost spiritually? How did God use your story for His glory?

_____

_____

_____

_____

Note: It is important that we learn from the story of Betsy, for future reference as life often brings detours. What does '*getting **lost** in Christ*' mean to you? I have listed below what it means to me:

- **Surrendering completely to His authority**
- **Following Christ's leading and desires above our own**
- **Giving Christ glory in each aspect of our lives**
- **Choosing to allow Him full-access to our daily schedules (even when unexpected detours happen)**

How might God use your 'scotch tape'?

_____

_____

_____

_____

Prayer: "Father, teach me to be a kind-hearted woman. Order the course of my days, according to your will. I long to get lost in You. Lovingly teach me to notice others." Amen.

CHAPTER SEVEN

JOY

Our past hurts often paralyze us. Becoming a woman of interior elegance requires giving all past painful experiences over to Christ, knowing He can be trusted with each one. He will use our greatest hurt for a greater glory than we can ever imagine. Joy is hard to hold onto when our circumstances in life threaten to undo us. I have witnessed women in their forties, fifties, even seventies—still holding onto childhood pains and grudges. Many have become emotionally frozen in time.

For many years, I could not look at my third-grade picture without being taken back to a painful childhood experience. Glancing at the faded photograph, you might see a joy-filled third grader. When I look at my picture, I see embarrassment and pain attached to the memory of that day. My hair was pulled back in the center of my head and neatly clipped with a small barrette. My head cocked to one side, shoulders lifted up toward my chin, and a big grin exposing my rotten baby teeth. Bunny rabbit teeth, protruding front and center, seemed to fight for attention.

The teacher held the picture high in the air so that everyone was sure to get a glance. Laughter filled the room as some twenty-four children and one teacher cackled together in brutal harmony. They giggled, sneered, and looked my way.

I folded my arms just in time for my little head to fall into the cradle they created, hiding my face. I wished to escape.

Shame and sadness created a small puddle of tears on the desktop. For the first time in my short life, I was embarrassed of my smile and vowed from that day forward not to smile in another school picture ever again. I didn't until five years later in my eighth grade picture.

I recall that day from time to time. Although painful, I am thankful for what it taught me. It taught me at a very young age what it means to be hurt and what it feels like to be made fun of. I resolved to try very hard to not make someone else feel that way.

What I learned from that experience has proven powerful. We can choose to be better because of persecution, not worse. But it is a choice we must make. We must intentionally choose not to be *embittered* by the situations and circumstances we face in our lives.

For many years, my joy was robbed because of someone else's wrongdoing. I allowed that painful occasion to ultimately change the way I felt around people, becoming overly self-conscious. I didn't want to smile wide enough for my rotten little teeth to show ever again.

We all have them—those *rotten* places that affect our self-esteem. Did someone's cruel words affect you so negatively that you are emotionally frozen in time? Have you allowed someone to rob your joy and take your smile away? Is the hurt so deep that you fear you may never be the same again? Christ wants to take the brokenness and sadness away forever and give you back your smile. It will not happen overnight, but in time—it surely will happen, and when it does, your joy will burst forth in a way you never thought possible. When this healing comes, the rest of the world may continue to laugh but it will not affect you in the same way, for your confidence will be in Him. Those 'rotten teeth,' hurt-filled areas of your life will not have power over you again. So, jump for joy and smile, my friend—smile real big!

$\mathcal{D}$

THE ELEGANT WOMAN OF GOD SEEKS TO FIND TRUE JOY.

Be joyful always; pray continually.
1 Thessalonians 5:16 (NIV)

ELEGANT REFLECTIONS

Reread Thessalonians 5:16. How does our prayer-life help in finding and keeping lasting joy?

_____

_____

_____

_____

Has someone ever hurt you so deeply, it paralyzed you emotionally?

_____

_____

_____

_____

Have you forgiven that person? Forgiveness is the gift we give to ourselves. It frees us, releases us, and heals us. (In the space below write an honest prayer asking God to help you forgive.)

_____

_____

_____

_____

When we allow others to rob us of our joy, we have little strength to face each day. Bitterness turns us into something very ugly. In what way can you identify with this?

_____

_____

_____

_____

List your major 'joy-robbers' below. Surrender each one to the power of God:

———————————————————————————————
———————————————————————————————
———————————————————————————————
————————————————————————

Make a new commitment below to let go of bitterness and animosity:

———————————————————————————————
———————————————————————————————
———————————————————————————————
————————————————————————

> *Prayer: "Father, reveal to me any unforgiving attitude. Free me. Help me to use the pain I have experienced as a powerful tool to identify with others and bring glory to your name. Turn every bitter memory into something better. I long to experience the fullness of joy found only in you."*
>
> *Amen.*

CHAPTER EIGHT

WHEN JOY LEAVES TOWN

When you wake up each morning, is your mind preoccupied with the matters of the day? Do you sometimes find your heart heavy with a load of worry and/or regret? What do you do with all the cares you carry deep within the pockets of your heart? Do you hold on with both hands, gripping the things you want to control, the things you wish to somehow *fix*? Control is a battle for us all. We burden ourselves by worrying, instead of trusting God. His strength is perfect in our weaknesses.

What do you do?

- **When your co-worker dies at age thirty-six of a massive heart attack, leaving behind a lovely wife who is pregnant with their second child.**
- **When someone you love is battling cancer, chemotherapy and the uncertainty of tomorrow.**

- When your father has Parkinson's disease and prostate cancer, and your mother is exhausted from caring so lovingly for him.
- When you live eight hours away from someone hurting and realize you cannot be there to give support the way you would like.
- When someone you love is deeply depressed or oppressed by the darkness overshadowing their mind, and no feeble attempt on your part helps to lighten their load.
- When someone you love is severely addicted to drugs or alcohol, is bulimic, anorexic or bound to some other addiction.
- When you want to be married more than anything else in the world and for whatever reason, the Lord has not granted your wish.
- When your dream of giving birth is dashed because of irreparable medical conditions.
- When the bills are piled high and you have lost your job, unsure how you will ever make ends meet.
- When you get the call that your son has just been killed in a car accident.
- When your family is grown and gone and your spouse is deceased, and you sit alone by the window reminiscing of days gone by.
- When joy has packed her bags and left town and you fear she may never visit your house again.

The path is not easy, but you are not fighting this battle alone. All trials will melt away when His great light is revealed. The hope of someday standing in the glory of the Lord will carry you through the most joyless day. Cling to joy. Cling to hope. Strive toward developing an elegant, godly character. Don't ever give up. Don't ever give in. Christ is with you. He will hold your hand with each step you take.

For I am the Lord your God who takes hold of your right hand and says to you, "Do not fear; I will help you." Isaiah 41:13 (NIV)

If you feel joy is too far from your reach, you are correct! But the good news is this: nothing is beyond His reach. So stand on the front porch and look for your strong friend, Joy. Wait for her expectantly. It is only when we look for joy that we are able to find her. When she does arrive, invite her in and throw open the windows. Let the fresh breeze of this new strength flow from your house into the hearts of others who may also be struggling to make it through the day.

THE ELEGANT WOMAN IS JOYFUL AND STRONG!

The joy of the Lord is my strength. Nehemiah 8:10 (NIV)

ELEGANT REFLECTIONS

Have you ever experienced a life-altering moment when you lost your joy because the circumstances seemed too much to bear?

_____
_____
_____
_____

List the pains you have not fully given to God. Surrender them here and allow Him to help you heal.

_____
_____
_____
_____

Reread Nehemiah 8:10 (NIV): *The joy of the Lord is my strength.* How does our joy-level affect our strength each day?

_____
_____
_____
_____

What happens to us when we focus our attention more on the stressful circumstances of life?

_____
_____
_____
_____

Reread Isaiah 41:13 (NIV): *For I am the Lord your God who takes hold of your right hand and says to you, do not fear; I will help you.*

What hope do you find in this promise?

_____

_____

_____

_____

As we continue on our journey, striving diligently to become women of interior elegance, fear is turned to faith. Do you see this happening in your life? If not, write the fearful struggles you are facing on the lines below. Surrender each one to the authority of Christ's power and watch Him strengthen you:

_____

_____

_____

_____

Prayer: "Father, I want to thank you for the promise that you will take hold of my right hand today, and every day of my life. I know I can trust you. Help me to live in your power instead of living in the pain of my circumstances. I know you have a good plan for me and you will not waste anything. Fill me with joy and strength."

Amen.

CHAPTER NINE

LISTEN...HE IS SPEAKING

Did you know the Lord intercedes for you daily? There was a time when only the High Priest could enter into the most holy place where God's spirit dwelled. The high priest offered sacrifices, asking for the sins of the people to be forgiven. But Christ's death on the cross allowed each of us to enter into a sacred intimacy with him through prayer. We no longer need a high priest to represent us because Christ left us the gift of his Holy Spirit, who now intercedes on our behalf before the throne of God. When we accept Christ as our savior, we are given the sweet privilege of making our requests known to Him. At anytime, day or night, we can whisper our deepest desires and concerns into His holy ears. He then, goes before the Father on our behalf, interceding and representing us to the Holy of Holies.

I don't know about you, but I am honored. To think the Holy Spirit whispers our deepest heart's desires into God's holy ears. I am amazed that, on our worst days when we cannot pray because the pain runs so deep, He lovingly prays for us. He sees the best in us and reminds the Lord of our potential. Imagine Him standing before the throne of God saying: *"Lord, aren't you proud of our daughter? See how hard she is trying to be refined and polished into OUR image? Forgive her Father, for all her shortcomings. Help her Father. Teach her to live the life you intend for her good. Father, she knows not what she does."*

When we are tempted to be critical of ourselves and others, and are tempted to judge others harshly, He is compassionate, loving, and kind. He sees to the core of our hearts and chooses to love us anyway.

We do not have to live life alone, friend. But we must learn to listen to the voice of our Heavenly Father. Let's allow His spirit to refine us, polish us, mold us and shape us into mighty prayer warriors. Even if you don't know how to pray, He will teach you how to pray. He wants you to talk to Him daily as you would talk to a best friend: pour your heart out, share with him every care and concern, and feel the sweet release of surrender. As you cast your cares upon Him, you become free in your heart and mind. Then you can freely and powerfully pray for the cares and concerns of others.

A woman of interior elegance intercedes for her family. Intercessory prayer is important. We are told in the word of God to pray for one another in love. There is no set formula. There is no perfect way of stringing words together. All we have to do is come before Him humbly, making our requests known. He is a loving Father, a best friend, and an intercessor for those who put their faith in His omnipotent power. An elegant woman of God understands her need for prayer. She also understands the power of prayer. She selflessly fights for her family, on her knees.

When I was a young girl, my Daddy prayed every night for our family. While he prayed, we wiggled, giggled, and made faces at each other. This did not stop his fervency. He kept praying with great intention, no matter how uninterested we children were. I remember the temptation to look around the room while everyone else had their eyes closed. Perhaps it was a good thing because I have the memory of my mother and father, on their knees in prayer, etched in my mind to this day. Those nights when Daddy led our family in prayer are some of my most treasured memories. I am so thankful for my earthly Mother and Father who taught me how to pray.

This happened nightly at the Roland house, and this tradition continued to be special in my family. I wish I could tell you it happened every night. It didn't. But each time we did pray, I know power came down as our prayers were lifted up, whether on our knees or upright. I am convinced the power of prayer is often unseen, at least right away. Many of the prayers my Mother and Father prayed have been answered years later.

After getting married and having a family of my own, I found myself captivated each time my precious husband and children dropped to their knees in prayer. As I said earlier, it did not happen every night as it did when I was growing up. But, what is important is it *did* happen. Please keep in mind, my elegance-seeking sister, it is not the number of times we pray, or the posture in which we pray that matters most. It is about having a willing heart to commune with God, listen to Him, and exercise faith. It is about believing He will hear and answer our prayers. It is about trusting Him, even when we can't understand His ways.

Please don't allow the enemy to cause you to live in regret or feel like a failure if you didn't physically get down on your knees with your children each and every night. Perhaps you realize you fell short in praying with, and for, your family. I want to encourage you to focus on what you have done right, instead of what you have done wrong. Today marks a brand new day. Is this the first time you have ever prayed? How exciting! God is listening whenever you call out to Him. Lift each of your family members up to Him now. Call each of their names aloud. Things are changing in the heavenly realm, even when your eyes cannot see instant results. He will teach you how to pray. Listen carefully.

We are empty nesters now. Believe me when I say the enemy rushes in daily, seeking to destroy memories. But when I walk into our family room, it is easy to remember those nights of family prayer. Tears fill my eyes as I look around the empty room—memories of our oldest son, on his knees by the old, worn-out sofa flash before me. I can still see his big, strong body there on his knees before God. Oh, what a beautiful sight—sweet images remain etched in my heart of our daughter, kneeling quietly beside me with her long, beautiful hair sweeping forward as her head is bowed in prayer. I look across the room where our youngest son, kneeled. His small body a perfect, pint-sized clone of the man I married. I can recall in a moment how sweet he looked while kneeling silently with his little hands clasped in prayer.

There were times of wiggling and giggling, just as I had done—but eventually, a captive audience. At times it appeared they were barely breathing, wanting to hear their father's gentle voice in prayer. They soaked in every word. I recognized in my spirit why my own children were so silent and still, for I too, fell quiet and still when I heard my father's voice in prayer. The giggling and wiggling were forced to stop by the power in the room. It was the most edifying time of my life. I knew 'Daddy' would call out my name. He would ask God to bless me and to walk with me through my life. He would often pray aloud his thoughts concerning me personally— whispering things I had done or said— drawing attention to specific things he had noticed and appreciated. Often it would be an acknowledgment of growth he had noticed taking place in my spiritual life. It moved my heart so much, as he pointed out things in my character that I had never noticed in myself. His words were the kindest things said of me, that I had ever heard. I drew them into my very being—allowing each word to wash over my motionless body. It was during those nights of prayer that my faith and confidence grew as I gained an understanding of my Savior's love for me. I knew if my father spoke it, it must be true.

Perhaps you did not have this blessing of seeing your spouse or your own earthly father praying on your behalf. Maybe you never heard one edifying sentence lifted up with your name attached to it. Perhaps few or no words of love ever flowed from the lips of the one from whom you most needed to hear them. Well, my dear friend, I can assure you there is one who loves you deeply. You are important to Him. He knows everything about you and loves you, no matter what you have or have not done. His name is Jesus. He whispers your name daily to God the Father. He has good, edifying things to say about you. His words are so gentle and full of love. He sees the intent of your heart. Even now He is there at the Father God's throne, whispering your name, speaking edifying words about you. He praises God for *your* life for through you, He is being revealed to others. He prays for your strength and courage.

If you will stop wiggling and take the time to sit quietly in His presence, you just might hear Him speaking. His voice is the most edifying, loving voice ever to speak over you. He will reveal good things about you that you have never seen in yourself. For when the Father speaks, you can rest assured that His words are true. So don't move a muscle, be still–be very, very still.

The Father has something to say.

THE ELEGANT WOMAN OF GOD PRAYS.

My Intercessor is my friend. Job 16:20 (NIV)

The prayer of a righteous man (woman) is powerful and effective.
James 5:16 (NIV)

ELEGANT REFLECTIONS

What does it mean to be an intercessor?

_____

_____

_____

_____

What does it mean to you to know that Jesus, the Son of God, is interceding for you in the courts of heaven?

_____

_____

_____

_____

Reread Job 16:20 (NIV): *My Intercessor is my friend.* Have you ever thought of Jesus as your friend?

_____

_____

_____

_____

How might viewing Jesus as your friend change the way you view your relationship with Him?

_____

_____

_____

_____

Do you practice listening for the voice of the Lord in your own life each day? Write about a time when you clearly heard the voice of your friend, Jesus, speaking to you.

_____

_____

_____

_____

Read the following scripture verse: *When you pray, go into your room, close the door and pray to your Father, who is unseen. Then your Father, who sees what is done in secret, will reward you.* Matthew 6:6 (NIV)

How often do you practice going into a private place to pray. How does this scripture verse challenge you?

_____

_____

_____

_____

Prayer: "Father, speak to me. Quiet me in your holy presence; settle my anxious heart. Help me to listen for your voice, and follow your wise counsel. Thank you for interceding for me. Teach me to be a woman of prayer who willingly intercedes for others." Amen.

Chapter Ten

MY INTERIOR DECORATING FRIEND

I remember clearly the first time He came to my home. My nerves were on edge because I knew that He was an authority on interior design. I was afraid of the criticism I would face: afraid He would criticize my best efforts.

It wasn't that way at all.

As He stepped inside, peace washed over me. It was like a calming wind had gently blown through my home, pushing away any anxiety I had previously felt. *"You have a lovely home. It is unique. You are the only one with a home exactly like this. That makes it really special,"* he softly said.

He began to study the walls, going from room to room at a slow, even pace. There were areas of darkness where he added just the right light, but then the light exposed more need.

"It's time for a change and I am just the man to help you."

He gently reminded me that it was way past time to move out of my comfort zone.

He drew my attention to a table that I had draped with a bold, beautiful fabric. I wanted to cover it because it was so damaged. He pulled the cloth away, exposing the table for what it was. There it was in plain light. I was ashamed. Scratches and indentations screamed imperfection.

He eased my embarrassment when He said, *"Oh, you mustn't cover this; it is a thing of beauty. It could be used to help others identify with you in a way that they never could if you cover it. You see, someone may see the table and identify with the scars it has collected from years of past abuse. It's authentic - real. No, don't hide this one. Its scars are its true beauty."*

He pointed toward my bookshelves. Boy, did I have quite a collection! There were many that I didn't even remember I'd accumulated. There were books on anger, bitterness, envy, jealousy, greed, gossip, and unforgiveness. One was entitled: *How to Have a Pity Party, and Like It*. There were many quick reference guides to things such as: *How to Hurt Someone as Badly as They Have Hurt You (And Then Some)*. There were scads of history books: *Get Back and Get Even; Jealously Over Godliness; Verbal Stabs That Kill; Hug Your Hurt Like a Teddy Bear; Snuggle into Sin;* and *Make a Quilt Out of Guilt*. His eyes scaled the shelves. He slowly and gently began to remove them. He said they were cluttered and of no use to me or to my guests. He began to replace them with books regarding love, joy peace, patience, goodness, kindness, and self-control. He said history just wasn't His thing, that he was more interested in my future than my past; the books he recommended would bring me a future and a hope.

I was amazed at how he took my old stuff and rearranged it. He made each room seem new and more inviting, the kind of room where anyone who needed rest could snuggle.

He continued through my house hanging new mirrors. He said I had only been able to see distorted reflections of myself. His was a *New Image* mirror, the best quality–guaranteed to reflect a true image, as He sees me. It would show me how beautiful I really am, from His perspective. He lovingly pointed out that what was on the interior of my home would reflect outwardly, whether I wanted it to, or not. He was there to take care of any junk that would hinder my joy.

I cringed with embarrassment when He lifted the rug in my hallway. I was angry. I remember thinking, *"I invited Him here to do the work I wanted Him to do–He's taking it a bit too far!"* There it was in plain view, the mound of dirt I had swept under the rug. Things I didn't want anyone to know about. I wanted them to think my house was perfectly elegant, twenty-four hours a day. I could no longer vainly attempt to impress Him. He had exposed the dirtiest part of my home. His indescribable light spread across my rubble of brokenness. He didn't laugh or tease me. But, He didn't clean it up for me either. Instead, He gently gave wisdom, teaching me how to bring order to my house of chaos. Even though my heart was willing to change, I had no idea where to start because I was overwhelmed. He told me if I lacked wisdom, all I had to do is ask Him for it, and He would give generously to me without finding fault. (James 1:5-NIV)

He opened the closet, the place into which I had thrown all my clutter; things I thought were unworthy and useless. I was shocked by how much had accumulated over the years. I shrunk back as my insecurities spilled out, forming a huge mound on the floor. There were gifts and talents that were God-given, yet I had stored them away carelessly. I wasn't willing to take the risk of using them for fear of rejection or failure, so I had thrown them in the closet along with everything else. My pride was in danger. Hiding seemed easier than being subjected to the scrutiny of some critical soul.

He organized the closet in a way that it had never been before. First, He separated the good from the bad. Then, He separated the old from the new. He was a master at this. I sensed my deep need for Him and could feel myself loosening my grip on control. Before I knew it, He had purged my entire house. He gently discarded things cluttering His path. Then revealed treasures I had perceived as trash.

He opened all the windows in my home. *"Your home is filled with rare finds and they must be shared with all who come near, for they are not yours alone,"* He calmly stated.

He wasn't there just to decorate my home. He wanted the keys, the deed—full ownership. He said He could teach me how to be an interior decorator also. He would show me how to decorate the homes of dear friends and strangers by administering grace to them and loving them unconditionally. He said I must embrace my home before I could fully embrace others.

If you are in need of some interior decorating, I would be happy to give you a referral—

my friend, Jesus Christ: a professional in every sense of the word, a specialist in restoration, and very creative because His Father is the greatest creator of all time. His service is free. He is available to come into your home for daily consultations. He redeems, rejuvenates, and restores. He desires that we live our lives as though His reputation depended on it.

Allow Him to teach you how to become a woman of interior elegance. Make an interior decorating appointment with Him today.

THE ELEGANT WOMAN OF GOD WELCOMES THE RENEWING POWER OF GOD.

That you may walk worthy of the Lord, fully pleasing Him, being fruitful in every good work and increasing in knowledge of God. Colossians 1:10 (NIV)

ELEGANT REFLECTIONS

Many women resist change. Do you welcome or resist change?

_____

_____

_____

_____

Letting go of control is key to becoming a woman of interior elegance. List a few things that come to your mind that you might not have surrendered.

_____

_____

_____

_____

As you read the preceding chapter, *My Interior Decorating Friend,* what things did you realize you need to allow Christ to remove, change, restore, or redeem?

_____

_____

_____

_____

What spoke to you most in the story about My Interior Decorating Friend?

_____

_____

_____

_____

Reread Colossians 1:10: *That you may walk worthy of the Lord, fully pleasing Him, being fruitful in every good work and increasing in knowledge of God.* Write in the space below how this speaks to you.

_____

_____

_____

_____

Prayer: "Father, I surrender my controlling nature to you. Change me from the inside out. Do the interior decorating you see fit. I trust you. I pray you will rearrange, redeem, and restore the old cluttered places in my heart. I want to be a woman of interior elegance." Amen.

Chapter Eleven

PANSY MOMENTS

It's not every day that a person has the opportunity to experience what I like to call a *'pansy moment.'*

I had driven past the beautiful pansy garden at the front of our subdivision every day for the entire season and yet, I had never paid much attention to them. It is amazing how the Lord has a way of drawing us back to the basics. It usually takes tough situations or some hard knocks in life to teach us real truths and make us stop to smell the roses, or in this case, the pansies.

This had been a hard knock kind of week. My heart was heavy with the news of my father's declining health as well as my mother-in-law's reoccurring cancer. I felt trapped in a crazy, fast-paced schedule and longed to slow down. Maybe that is why I so intently took notice of the pansies on this particular day. I found myself longing to stop and pick a bouquet of them. It was such a compelling flowerbed with a magnetic force. Perhaps I somehow thought they would help to cheer me up a bit.

Three days passed. I basically kept the same routine. I drove past the pansies each day with a deep longing to stop and pick them, yet I was too busy. On this particular day, as I drove down the street to where our home is located, something caught my eye. There in the street, just in front of our mailbox, I noticed a beautiful bouquet of flowers.

After parking the car, I walked quickly toward the flowers, anxious to confirm what I already knew. Reaching down, I saw they were in fact pansies: perfectly clustered together, bluntly cut on the end as if delivered by a florist, a beautiful, perfect bouquet! The colors were bursting forth in electric shades of blue, yellow, orange, purple and gold.

With tears streaming down my face like fresh spring rain, my face now turned upward toward the morning sunlight, I praised the Lord for sending me a bouquet of pansies. I felt so loved and warm inside as I fully embraced the moment of this miracle.

Soon I began to question, doubting such a thing could have happened at all. *Who would be up so early picking pansies?* I had not shared my desire to pick the pansies with anyone. *How did they get there? Am I dreaming? I must be going nuts! I must be exhausted! This simply could not be! There must be some explanation!*

As my children came home from school, I asked each of them if they had picked a bouquet of pansies and put them in front of the mailbox. They looked at me like I was crazy and reminded me how early in the morning they leave for school. I walked out to the end of our driveway and down the street to see which of my neighbors had pansies planted in their yard. I remember thinking that maybe one of them had picked the flowers on their morning walk and accidentally dropped them in the street on their way home. Not one neighbor had pansies growing in their yard.

When my husband came home for dinner, I asked him if he had picked any flowers before leaving to take the children to school. He also looked at me like I was really losing it. After all, he is a rough-and-tough kind of outdoorsman. He is most definitely not the early morning, pansy- picking type of guy. I had failed to remember the fact that it is dark outside when he leaves to go to work during the winter months.

I could not stop thinking about the beautiful bouquet. I thought about how my first instinct was to embrace them as a miracle from the Lord, but then the doubting began. The Holy Spirit started to deal with my heart, reminding me of the miracles Jesus performed and recorded throughout His word. I remembered how: He had healed the blind man and caused him to see, how He walked on the water, how He made the lame to walk, caused the dumb to speak. I recalled the stories of how He turned the water into wine, and multiplied the loaves and the fish in order to feed the multitude. I thought of what a miracle it was that a virgin could give birth to a Savior, how He died on the cross, and then rose again after being sealed in a tomb for dead. Each recollection ripped my heart into shreds and made me feel such shame for having doubted that the same God who did all of these mighty things, and so much more, could have His angels deliver to me a bouquet of pansies.

It was then that I heard that still, small voice inside of me, the voice of the Holy Spirit, speaking, *"La-'Tan, if those who experienced the miracles I performed long ago would have chosen not to believe, if they had been afraid to share the things they witnessed, or questioned them in disbelief, my Word (the Living Bible) might have never been written. If I am the same God yesterday, today, and forever, do I not have the power to work miracles still today if I so choose?"*

"Okay Lord, now I am getting it. Now, I truly hear you."

Since that day, I have believed in miracles with the faith of a little child. I try very hard not to question life's unexplainable blessings that come my way, but instead, actively seek 'pansy moments' each and every day. I am sure I miss them sometimes, especially on days when I am caught up in selfish preoccupations.

I want to challenge you to embrace each day fully as a true miracle from the Lord. After all, there are no coincidences, just God incidences.

Look for them–those little, unexpected miracles that God wants to reveal on a daily basis. Keep your eyes open. Look closely. There just might be a special delivery coming your way. This might be a 'pansy moment' kind of day!

THE ELEGANT WOMAN OF GOD IS A *SEEKER*.

You will seek me and find me when you seek me with all your heart.
Jeremiah 29:13 (NIV)

ELEGANT REFLECTIONS

Have you ever experienced a 'pansy moment?'

_____
_____
_____
_____

Think about the days you have lived distracted by your circumstances instead of actively seeking Christ in your life. What was the major difference you noticed in the way your day went?

_____
_____
_____
_____

Reread Jeremiah 29:13 (NIV): *You will seek me and find me when you seek me with all your heart.*

How might we seek Christ in our daily lives?

_____
_____
_____
_____

How might we find Christ in our daily lives?

_____
_____
_____
_____

What do you think it means to seek Christ with all our heart?

_____

_____

_____

_____

What challenged you most in the preceding chapter, entitled: *Pansy Moments?*

_____

_____

_____

_____

Prayer: "Father, teach me to seek you each day. I desire more of you and less of me. Today, I rededicate my heart to you. Make me aware of you. Give me the heart of a true seeker. Help me to notice the big and small blessings you give to me each day." Amen.

Chapter Twelve

PLAYING DRESS UP

My mother's dress hung off my small shoulders, puddling on the floor behind me. My crown was cocked sideways on my small head. Tiny toes gripped into the pointed, high-heel pump shoes as I walked clumsily down the hall into the family room. I posed proudly in front of my father's big chair. He smiled at me, his gentle blue eyes sparkling. He looked on with pride as I twirled around in small circles, the fabric wrapping itself around my small ankles. In my mind, I was gliding gracefully but the truth was plain to see.

"How do I look, Daddy?" I asked, knowing full well what he would say.

"Oh, Monkey, you look so pretty!"

My little heart would leap for joy. My father knew how unrealistic it was for me to even think I could fill my mother's dress and shoes. He knew I had much growing to do, and that I had a long way to go. Yet he still smiled at me, as if to say he was pleased with my childish efforts.

My Heavenly Father is there, in the courts of heaven, sitting in His big chair - His throne. I come before Him daily in prayer: my crown is cocked sideways on my head, my dress is hanging off my shoulders, and the train is dragging behind me as my toes grip forward into shoes much too large. He smiles at me with his gentle eyes, knowing how hard I am trying to fill shoes much too large for me at this point in my walk with Him. He is so proud of me anyway. He is pleased with my efforts. He knows in His wisdom that I am growing.

Someday, when I walk down the hallway of heaven to meet Him sitting there on His throne, He will smile with a twinkle in His eye as He says to me, "Oh, my daughter, you are so beautiful. I am enthralled by your beauty. Well done."

He will give me a new robe that fits perfectly and will straighten the crown on my head. My twirling will be done. I can rest in Him forever. I need not seek approval from anyone else. I will have His full attention.

𝒟

THE ELEGANT WOMAN OF GOD FINDS HER AFFIRMATION IN CHRIST.

See, I have engraved you on the palms of my hands. Isaiah 49:16 (NIV)

ELEGANT REFLECTIONS

Where do you find your affirmation?

_____

_____

_____

_____

The word of God has much to say about you. As you study His word, you will read edifying, encouraging words. The power of God's holy word will lift you up above the undone circumstances of your life. Devise a reading/study plan on the lines below:

_____

_____

_____

_____

Reread Isaiah 49:16 (NIV): *See, I have engraved you on the palms of my hands.*

God has your name engraved on the palm of His holy hands. What does this mean to you?

_____

_____

_____

_____

Think about the people you have 'twirled and danced' for in order to gain their affirmation. What was the end result? Did you feel affirmed?

_____

_____

_____

_____

As we continue on our journey to become women of interior elegance, we will find ourselves longing to dance and twirl only to an audience of ONE-Jesus Christ, the Son of the living God.

On the following lines, rededicate yourself to focusing your attention each day on what pleases Christ.

_____

_____

_____

_____

I want to challenge you to practice resting in Christ's love for you. Ask Him to reveal His heart concerning your life. He finds you worthy. He will faithfully clothe you in righteousness and beauty.

_____

_____

_____

_____

Prayer: "Father, I commit myself to dancing to an audience of ONE today – YOU! I pray you will teach me to rest in you fully. I love you, Father. Thank you for loving me and for finding me worthy." Amen.

CHAPTER THIRTEEN

REMOVING THE MASKS

No more pretending, friend. It is time to get real with God. It is time to take off the mask. From this day forward, let's agree to do away with false pretenses. How exhausting it is trying to please others. Too often, we focus more energy on pleasing those who don't have our best interest at heart, than on those who do. The people who are our biggest cheerleaders often take a backseat to those mean-spirited, less-deserving people.

We want everyone to love us, or at least like us. Most of us aren't willing to admit our need to be loved and accepted. The desire to be loved is a normal part of being human, but we create misery for ourselves when we mask who we really are in an attempt to be accepted by others. No wonder we are a tired, sad, and depressed generation of women. We have worked so hard to project an unrealistic image of perfection.

In II Corinthians 13:11, we are told to aim for perfection. The perfection we are to aim for is not the perfection of man, but the perfection of a loving God who transforms a willing woman's heart into the perfect, elegant image He created her to be.

The masks we tend to wear are often for our own protection. Low self-esteem hinders us in multiple ways, demanding we shrink back, hide, and avoid being vulnerable. We often feel exposed if we allow others into the intimate places of our lives. The façade that everyone else's life is perfect, while ours is a mess, keeps our masks firmly in place.

I enjoy researching different topics in order to use off-the-cuff material for speaking events across the country. Recently, I researched chameleons. I learned that chameleons are a distinctive and highly specialized clade of lizards. As I read what Wikipedia had to say about chameleons, I saw an interesting parallel. It looks as if women have many lessons to learn from Miss Chameleon:

Lesson #1: Some scientists believe our friend, Miss Chameleon, changes color in order to blend into her environment.

I don't know about you, but on so many occasions, I have feverishly tried to blend into the world around me. Insecurities fed my need to camouflage myself—masking my true, authentic self, for fear of rejection. I didn't want to stand out too much because I had witnessed first-hand how confident women tend to make insecure women feel badly about themselves.

Christ's love enables a woman of interior elegance to look for opportunities to make everyone else feel important and special. You see, when ones heart is in line with the heart of God, one's goals are different. Instead of self-seeking, there is a desire to empower others to celebrate who they are. Little did I know, blending in was an act of insecurity; and like Miss Chameleon, a way to hide from enemy attack.

Each of us has been gifted with unique talents that are to be shared with the world around us. Sharing demands we take off our masks. Stand-up, stand-out, and celebrate who God made you to be. You are becoming a woman of interior elegance. You simply cannot afford to blend into the crowd. We are called to be set apart for God's glory and purpose. I have wasted so much time shrinking back from gifts and abilities.

I realized if I truly wanted to be an example, I must lead by example. Shrinking back or blending in with the world won't challenge others to strive for growth. And it surely won't help others pursue their God-given purpose.

Lesson #2: Other scientists disagree, saying Miss Chameleon changes color based on her mood, temperature, or light.

I laugh out loud at this one because I realize how often I have allowed my moods to change the way I presented myself in any given environment. Consistency should be the goal for all believers. I want to learn from Ms. Chameleon and work diligently to be consistent—not allowing my mood to dictate how I respond to people. No one likes to be around someone who is inconsistent. No one likes to feel the need to dip their toe into their loved one's emotional waters to test what the temperature is going to be for that given day.

Are you old enough to remember the Mood Ring fad? This ring had a stone which changed color based on body temperature, supposedly representing your mood. What if we could wear this stone on our forehead everyday as a way of announcing the mood we are in? Everyone would know when to stay away from us, right? Many of us wear an invisible Mood Ring, showing our true colors when the pressures of life start to squeeze. It would serve us well as believers to not be ruled by our bad moods. Wouldn't our best colors shine forth if we were intentional about walking in the fullness of God's light each day?

Lesson # 3: The chameleon's tongue is another interesting feature. The tip of its tongue is covered with a sticky secretion that grabs its prey. As they "shoot out" their long tongue (which can be as long as their body) they can have their prey in their mouth in a fraction of a second (faster than what the human eye can see). They can repeat the same action immediately after.

Whew! This fact really concerned me as I reevaluated my own tongue and how it functions on a daily basis. I wonder how many times my tongue has reached out in fury to grab, as prey, some innocent soul I felt led to gossip about. In reality, gossip is about us because it directly shows the condition of our hearts. A critical spirit is like the slimy tongue of our friend, Miss Chameleon, who grabs her prey and snatches it back into her mouth in the blink of an eye. As I studied this fact, I reflected back across twenty-nine years of marriage. I remembered, many times, speaking to my husband in unloving ways in an attempt to snatch him back into his rightful place, in accordance with my infinite wealth of wisdom and rightness. Then I would say to myself: *I am never going to respond that way to him again* - but much like my friend, the Chameleon, I found myself repeating the same action immediately after.

Lesson #4: *When frightened, the chameleon can make a hissing sound. They can bite (which is non-toxic and harmless).*

When you are frightened or angry, do you hiss or bite those whom you have been entrusted to love and bless? Perhaps you think your actions are harmless. Take note: although your bite isn't poisonous, it still causes pain and lingering bite marks that take time to heal. Be slow to speak in anger. Let your first response be prayer regarding struggles in any relationship. Otherwise, you will find yourself hissing and biting everyone in your path.

Let's learn big lessons today from Miss Chameleon. Let's be changed, not to blend in but to reflect the image of the most-high God. Let us be intentional about using our tongues to glorify the Father, who created us for His glory. Let's ask Him to give us confidence to step out, not shrink back or blend in with the world around us. Let us be set-apart for His service.

Lesson #5: *Chameleons' eyes have a unique quality, which is that they can rotate independently of the other: while one eye looks forward, the other can look back. This helps them to keep 'an eye' on their surroundings, and be alert and aware of danger. Their vision is known to be their best feature.*

I chuckle when I think of how many days I have wasted, looking back over my shoulder to the past. I am not sure how I managed to stay focused on the path ahead of me while simultaneously rolling one eye back to view my past (like a chameleon).

How much time do you spend looking back to days gone by? Do you find yourself living in regret, laced with feelings of failure? *"I should've, I could've, and I wish I would've"*—these were a few of the voices that met me there on the rocky road leading to my past. Friend, keep your eyes fixed on the path before you. Good days are ahead of you. But if, like the chameleon, you are tempted to roll an eye backwards, let it be done only for the purpose of celebrating where you came from in order to move forward in faith, knowing God will continue to take care of you.

Lesson #6: The chameleon walks with very slow, deliberate movements.

Let us walk with slow, deliberate movements toward the purpose and call on our lives, while listening to the voice of the Lord who will give us wisdom for each appropriate response. Let us use our tongue to praise the One who gave us life. Let us celebrate the gifts in others, instead of finding fault in them. Let us stand up and stand out for the purpose of representing Christ well. Let us reflect the colors of His love each day and be found consistent. Let us not waste another day blending in to the world around us. Let us look back only to remember how far we have come and how blessed we have been.

THE ELEGANT WOMAN OF GOD IS CONSISTENT.

Therefore, my dear brothers and sisters, stand firm. Let nothing move you. Always give yourselves fully to the work of the Lord, because you know that your labor in the Lord is not in vain. Corinthians 15:58 (NIV)

ELEGANT REFLECTIONS

Lesson #1: Some scientists believe our friend, Miss Chameleon, changes color in order to blend into her environment.

What did you learn from Lesson #1?

_____

_____

_____

_____

Have you been guilty of wearing a mask? Why?

_____

_____

_____

_____

The elegant woman of God is consistent.

Why is this important?

_____

_____

_____

_____

Why is it important for Christians not to blend in with the world around them?

_____

_____

_____

_____

What have you been shrinking back from? Why have you been shrinking back?

_____

_____

_____

_____

Write in the space below three things you must change in order to represent your authenticity in Christ.

_____

_____

_____

_____

Lesson #6: The chameleon walks with very slow, deliberate movements. How deliberate is your walk with God? Do you approach your life slowly and deliberately or hap hazardously?

_____

_____

_____

_____

Prayer: "Father, give me courage to remove the mask I have been hiding behind. Help me to stand out for your glory. Give me courage to not blend into the crowd. I want to represent you well." Amen.

CHAPTER FOURTEEN

SHE STOOPED TO CONQUER

❦

"**M**om, they were whispering to one another about the birthday party. They didn't want me to hear because I am not invited," my daughter said with a trembling voice as tears filled her big, beautiful eyes.

My heart felt like it was breaking in half as I listened. "They are my best friends at school, Mom. Why would they not invite me?"

I reached out to hug her, our arms wrapping around each other tightly. As she buried her soft, tear-stained face into the curve of my neck—I remembered how this had been her crying spot since she was a baby. We held each other without speaking a word. Sometimes, there are no words to make things better, so I cried with her.

One week later, while driving our daughter to school, she asked her dad in a quiet voice if he would please stop at the grocery store.

"Why Da-Nae'? Do you need something for school?"

"Well, sort of."

"What do you need, honey, because we already going to be late?"

"I need to buy a balloon for someone who is having a birthday party tonight."

"Who is it?" I asked.

"Do you remember the girl who was whispering about her birthday party in front of me? Well, I want to take a balloon to school for her."

I looked over at my husband and he looked at me, each of our hearts melting, both with a sense of pride and of sadness. We knew we had to stop even if it meant we would be late. It was worth it!

Da-Nae' walked happily into the grocery store and in a few moments, she came running out with a huge grin spread across her seventh-grade face. Her balloon was flying high in the air with a pack of chewing gum tied to the ribbon hanging from the bottom, acting as a weight. She was the happiest girl in the world.

My husband and I were so blessed by our daughter's actions that morning. She stooped to conquer feelings that could have been feelings of anger and hurt. Some people might ask why she would make a fool out of herself after being treated the way she was or how she could lower herself after what her friend had done to her, but when Christ is in the center of our lives, He empowers us to do things we could never do in our own human nature. She chose not to be a martyr. She chose to stoop a little so she could rise up on a much higher level. She chose to reject her sadness about not being invited to the party, and rise to a better occasion. The blessing of stooping to conquer her negative emotions enabled her to bless her friend, in spite of how she had been treated.

When was the last time you *stooped to conquer?*

THE ELEGANT WOMAN OF GOD STOOPS TO CONQUER.

Submit to one another out of reverence for Christ. Ephesians 5:21 (NIV)

ELEGANT REFLECTIONS

How do you respond when you are left out or mistreated? Be honest in the space below:

_____
_____
_____
_____
_____

Our goal is to become women of interior elegance. That means we break old ways of responding to painful encounters and intentionally establish new, godly behaviors. What behavior changes need to take place in your life?

_____
_____
_____
_____
_____

Reread Ephesians 5:21 (NIV): *Submit to one another out of reverence for Christ.*

How might we submit to one another in love? Does this apply only to those who treat us well?

_____
_____
_____
_____
_____

After reading *Stooping to Conquer*, what inspired you or challenged you most?

_____
_____
_____
_____
_____

Note: I have heard women say, "God doesn't expect me to be a door-mat. He doesn't expect me to allow people to walk on me." Stooping to Conquer doesn't mean we are to wear an invisible sign that says: ABUSE ME, I WILL STILL LOVE YOU. Instead, we are striving to allow the Holy Spirit control over our 'flesh girl.' Write down an area of struggle you need the Lord to help you 'stoop to conquer.'

_____
_____
_____
_____
_____

When was the last time you repaid evil with good?

_____
_____
_____
_____
_____

How did you feel?

_____
_____
_____
_____
_____

How does submitting to one another in love honor God?

_____

_____

_____

_____

_____

_____

Prayer: "Father, I surrender my old way of responding to you. I ask you to give me willingness to 'stoop to conquer' emotions that battle against my ability to make godly choices." Amen.

CHAPTER FIFTEEN

WOMEN OF INTERIOR ELEGANCE

I often reminisce about my grandmothers. Both of them were gentle, godly women who lived very simple lives. They served their families without complaining and took care of their households with grateful hearts. One of the things I most admire about my grandmothers was how they intentionally made no time for silly, meaningless arguments or pointless confrontations. They loved their family, their Lord Jesus, and the life they had been given. Both led quiet lives of integrity, truth, and honor. I don't remember ever hearing them speak an unkind word about anyone.

One of the greatest spiritual battles we will ever face as women is the struggle to control our emotions. Out-of-control emotions lead to an out-of-control tongue. As we continue on our journey to become women of interior elegance, we must practice self-control. Self-control is an important key to developing godly character. Self-control starts with one woman who is willing to make one right decision at a time. Each time we choose to respond the right way, Christ's transforming power can do the full work in us. Soon our '*flesh-girl*' will submit to the discipline of right choices.

My grandmothers were very good examples of self-control. How do you want others to remember you after you are gone from the earth? I want to be remembered as a peacemaker instead of a confrontational soul who tried to stir up trouble and force everyone to match my own opinion or agenda. I'd rather be busy tending to the needs of my own household than tempted to look into the windows of another in order to criticize them if they aren't living a life just like mine. I want to be re-membered as a gentle, kind, servant-hearted woman who spoke edifying things about others. I believe you want these things also.

How do we get there? We need a savior. We cannot do it alone. He will help us. All we have to do is ask.

Perhaps your examples have been far from Christ-centered ones. Maybe your memories consist of arguments around the dinner table, screaming matches, and fits of rage. You have the power to change the course of events going forward, sweet friend. Ask the Lord to help you retrain your way of responding.

Let's seek Christ today. Let's ask Him to establish new ways of com-municating. He will help us to live peaceful lives of integrity. Who knows, we might leave legacies for our children and grandchildren they deem worth writing about someday.

THE ELEGANT WOMAN OF GOD LIVES A BALANCED LIFE.

Make it your ambition to lead a quiet life, to mind your own business and to work with your hands, just as we told you, so that your daily life may win the respect of outsiders and so that you will not be dependent on anybody. 1
Thessalonians 4:11-12 (NIV)

ELEGANT REFLECTIONS

Do you struggle to control your emotions?

_____
_____
_____
_____

Do you lead a quiet, peaceful life or a chaotic, out-of-control life?

_____
_____
_____
_____

How did you feel challenged to grow and/or change after reading the preceding chapter entitled: *Women of Interior Elegance?*

_____
_____
_____
_____

Do you mind your own business or are you a 'Nosey Nelly'-needing to know the gossip on everyone in order to feel better about yourself?

_____
_____
_____
_____

Do you think others respect you? If so, what is it they see in your character? If not, what changes are you committed to make?

_____
_____
_____
_____

Reread 1 Thessalonians 4:11-12 (NIV): *"Make it your ambition to lead a quiet life, to mind your own business and to work with your hands, just as we told you, so that your daily life may win the respect of outsiders and so that you will not be dependent on anybody."*

In what way did the scripture verse above convict your heart?

_____

_____

_____

_____

What is your life ambition?

_____

_____

_____

_____

_____

_____

_____

_____

Prayer: *"Father, quiet me in your presence each day. Fill my home with your sweetness. I want to be about your business, Lord. Help me do away with selfish ambitions. Teach me to lead a quiet life that will win the respect of others. I want my life to bring you glory and honor."* Amen.

CHAPTER SIXTEEN

HER NAME IS DEPRESSION

She is lost inside a shell that is limp and lifeless. Her eyes cry out for help. She needs someone, anyone, to save her from her life of imprisonment. She cannot express her pain in words, but her eyes tell it all. They are the window to a history of brokenness. They are like stained glass: soft blue in color—streaked with broken red blood vessels—the result of a river of tears she has cried.

She seldom ever speaks. When you look into her eyes more closely, you can almost hear her screaming out for help. She sits staring into what appears to be space. In reality, her clouded mind keeps her locked inside a vault of shattered memories. Her heart is twisted and mangled by so many painful events—events that time won't erase. Sexual and physical abuse experienced have sealed her mind away from hope, convincing her that she will never find true joy.

The feelings of uselessness, guilt, and shame have left her emotionally crippled. Hopeless: a dark cloud leads her through her days and is a canopy over her as she tries to find sleep by night. Many times there is no sleep, for her restless state of mind keeps her in constant turmoil. She is alone and afraid. She would not share her dark pain even if she could for fear no one would understand; someone might blame her. The pain is too much to bear. It is a deep, gut-wrenching pain threatening to suck the last bit of life right out of her.

She waits for someone to make her feel the completeness she longs for, but no human being can. The weight of her heart would crush even the strongest person. She needs a savior who can lift her heavy load. Only Jesus Christ has the power. He alone took on all of her shame and disgrace when He carried her cross. Only He can give her true joy and reason to hope. Only He can make her feel worthy. Only He can unlock the vault of sadness and pain that have imprisoned her for so long. Only Jesus Christ has the power to shine the Father's great light into her dark world, and melt away all the evil shadows lurking behind her. Only Christ can mend her broken heart and give her a sound mind.

She tries to look beyond her life to someone else's, but self is in the way. Analyzing herself hinders her ability to *see* others—her own pain blocks her view. It is in dying to self that she will find true healing. Healing will begin at the moment when she gives Christ her all: the good, the bad, and the ugly. Then she will begin a new journey. She will look in front instead of behind. She will begin to look upward instead of downward.

You may be this lady of whom I am speaking, or you may know someone like her. If you are her, then stretch your weakened hands outward and upward—allowing Christ to help you stand. Come out of the darkness and into the light of His unconditional love. Pause for a moment. Linger in His presence. Feel His great love as it washes over your soul. Allow the cleansing, healing stream of His power to remove shame and blame. Embrace the brand new future He offers. As you seek, you will find it! As you find it, you will begin to live in freedom and possibility!

Depression does not define you! Healing is possible, my friend. Joy awaits you!

THE ELEGANT WOMAN OF GOD DOES NOT LIVE IN THE PAST.

"If you can," said Jesus. *"Everything is possible for him who believes."*
Mark 9:23 (NIV)

ELEGANT REFLECTIONS

Have you ever been depressed? What did it feel like?

_____

_____

_____

_____

After reading the preceding chapter entitled: _Her Name Is Depression,_ how could you relate?

_____

_____

_____

_____

Reread Mark 9:23 (NIV): _"If you can," said Jesus. "Everything is possible for him who believes."_

What does this mean?

_____

_____

_____

_____

Do you believe anything is possible for God? If so, write on the lines below what your need is:

_____

_____

_____

_____

Note: The word interior means inside. Becoming a woman of interior elegance doesn't mean we become internally self-centered, looking back to past regrets, living in defeat. Instead, we press forward, celebrating the blessings in our lives and the gift of others. A woman of interior elegance reaches outward. Instead of internalizing pain, she looks for ways to serve others. Serving others and praying prayers of thanksgiving are the best medicine for a depressed soul. How do you actively serve others?

_____
_____
_____
_____

How can serving others help ease our emotional pain?

_____
_____
_____
_____

Do you believe Christ's power can fill you with joy in the midst of your greatest pain?

_____
_____
_____
_____

Have you ever felt emotionally crippled? Write about it on the following lines:

_____
_____
_____
_____

The powers of hell cannot hold you captive when the power of Christ covers you. In order to find strength to fight against the powers of darkness, we must cling to the word of God. Are you willing to cling to the word of God—claiming it as the absolute authority over every struggle you face?

_____

_____

_____

_____

Prayer: "Father, pour your power over my deepest point of pain. Fill me with joy unspeakable. Renew my mind. Help me to become a woman of interior elegance, reflecting your light and hope to a world that is sad and depressed. I will choose to praise you in the pain. I thank you for the work you are doing in me." Amen.

Chapter Seventeen

STAND STILL. DON'T RUN!

I looked ahead and saw a great beast charging in my direction. Its head was enormous, saliva was dripping from its mouth, and blubber swayed with each step it took.

My daddy was a farmer in a very rural setting in Georgia, where I grew up. He raised pigs and sold them, or had them processed for sausage, ham and bacon for our family. It was an important means of income, as well as a means of providing meat for our family.

At times, the pigs would escape from their fenced area (the pigpen, as we called it) and run away. This was devastating to my father as it was a great monetary loss. This was one of many summer days that the pigs decided to see if the grass really was greener on the other side of the fence. After stomping through the fence, they ran crazily here and there. My daddy and brothers needed help, and so he handed my sister and me a large stick and instructed us to stand still should the pigs run toward us. He said that they would be intimidated by our refusal to move and would run in the other direction.

I was about ten years old at the time and some of the pigs weighed 400 pounds or more, level in height with my small shoulders.

I stood there, intent on following my daddy's instructions. Nothing would hinder my ten-year old determination. Then the pig approached and all at once, my courageous bravery melted away as my knees grew weaker and weaker. I raised my stick high in the air and slammed it down with full force across the large creature's head, now directly in front of me. I could hear sharp, shrill screaming and suddenly realized it was my own voice. When I lifted my stick into the air a second time, I realized it had broken down to nothing more than a nub. Fear overtook me. As I turned to run, I could hear the sound of my daddy's voice yelling in the distance, "Don't run, Monkey, whatever you do, don't run."

At that moment, I was so consumed by fear that his voice seemed more distant and muffled than ever as my small feet carried me faster and faster away.

Needless to say, that day ended in defeat for my daddy. It was a day that will be forever etched deep in my heart and mind because it made such a strong impression on my spiritual life and has been carried with me across the years, even into adulthood. I can almost see my daddy's beautiful, blue eyes meet mine again as he asked me later on that day, "Why did you run, Monkey?"

I hear my childhood voice reply, "My stick broke, it was not strong enough and I was afraid, Daddy."

My father's gentle response to my comment is the part that lingers still with me today. "Daddy would not let that pig hurt you. I was watching you. Don't you know I had a much bigger stick than yours?"

Since that day, there have been many times in my spiritual life when I felt as though Satan himself and his army were charging at me. I have often been afraid to stand still and strong with a courageous heart for fear I might be trampled. Many times, I have approached the battle-lines of my spiritual life with the wrong weapon of defense in hand. At the first sign of defeat, I ran in fear. If only I had remembered that my heavenly Father was near, His awesome power available to help as the charging enemy (Satan) threatened to trample me under his feet.

Perhaps you need to hear this today. Are you fighting your battles alone? Look now to the one who is the commander and chief. You do not have to face the battle ill equipped. He cares so deeply for you. He is looking on, even now. And, if you look closely, you might see that in His hand, He is holding a much larger stick than your own. He is there fighting your battles daily. His eyes are fixed on you and your charging enemy as well. He'll give you strength you never knew you had. So stand still, don't run! Whatever you do, my friend, *don't run!*

THE ELEGANT WOMAN OF GOD DOES NOT RUN FROM HER PROBLEMS.

No one will be able to stand up against you all the days of your life.
As I was with Moses, so I will be with you; I will never leave you or forsake you.
Joshua 1:5 (NIV)

ELEGANT REFLECTIONS

Perhaps you too, feel the enemy has been charging towards you. Write down what your greatest fear is.

_____

_____

_____

_____

Reread Joshua 1:5 (NIV): *"No one will be able to stand up against you all the days of your life. As I was with Moses, so I will be with you; I will never leave you or forsake you."*

How does this scripture verse comfort you?

_____

_____

_____

_____

In the same way fear kept me from focusing on my daddy's comforting voice, fear will paralyze you, if you let it. Listen for your Father's voice now. Allow Him to quiet you and calm you. What is He saying to you?

_____

_____

_____

_____

"Stand still, don't run!" How long have you been on the run, friend? Are you weary?

_____

_____

_____

_____

Note: When I hit the pig over the head with my small stick, it broke. I was not equipped to fight an enemy so powerful, but my daddy was! If I had realized my daddy had his eye on me and would not allow harm to come to me, I might have found courage to stand still.

Have you been fighting against the enemy in your own strength? Friend, you are not equipped, but your Father is! Claim Joshua 1:5. He will never leave you, nor forsake you! What does that mean to you?

_____

_____

_____

_____

Prayer: "Father, I have been running in fear for so long. I am weary. Help me stand strong. Remind me each day that I am not alone. You have your holy eyes on me and on every situation I will ever face in my life. You are powerful. The enemy cannot stand against your authority and greatness. Thank you for the promise to be with me."

Amen.

Chapter Eighteen

THE GIVING TREES

The year was 1984. I was to be married in June, fresh out of college and in a state of sheer glee. When your head is in the clouds, it is very hard to see all that is going on around you; I never really took notice of the financial strain my parents were under. My mom and dad grew up with little or no money to speak of, but were devoted to each other and to the Lord. They had always worked very hard to provide for our family. My dad was a farmer at the time, one of the hardest jobs known to mankind. He had poured himself into farming his whole life, working a secular job by day and farming by night, many times until the wee hours of the morning, six days a week.

He and Mom never told me how bad things were for them at the time because they didn't want to put a damper on my special wedding day. We picked out the cake and the dress; the whole wedding was now put together. They watched me with such love in their eyes as I stood in the doorway, modeling my wedding dress. They alone knew how fragile their financial situation was.

There had been several years of drought and crops weren't producing. Many farmers, like my dad, did not have access to irrigation systems to water their crops, so their loss was much greater. My dad was now sixty-one years old and in poor health. He should have been looking forward to retirement at that time in his life but because of their impending financial strain, retirement would not be on the radar for several years to come. Because he faithfully made all of his payments on-time, he had asked the bank for an extension on his loan—agreeing to pay the accumulated interest—until financial circumstances were better.

One day, shortly after my wedding, a man came to the door while my mother was home alone. He told her he wanted to come in and look at their house. Since she was home alone and did not know the man, she did not feel safe enough to let the man in. She told him that my dad would be home soon and he could come inside then. My dad was late getting home and the man grew impatient. He came to the door again, insisting that he had to come in. My mom asked if he could please come back another day. He then proceeded to come into the house against her wishes and told her they had one month to vacate the house.

After the man left, my mother wept as she closed the door to the home that held so many memories for us all. She recently shared with me that as she stood there with tears filling her eyes, she could almost hear my dad saying, "Time to go to church kids, get up." Then he would sing *Victory in Jesus* over and over again in his tenor voice until we couldn't stand hearing another verse and finally gave in and got out of bed. She could almost smell the scent of Sunday lunch cooking for the many people she had entertained across the years. As she glanced into the dining room, she could envision their smiling faces as they feasted on the meal she had lovingly poured her heart into. Many of these people were total strangers, visitors to the little country church we attended at the time. She had invited them on a whim while waiting just outside the church for them to make their exit. By the time the meal was completed, they felt like family because of her gift of love and hospitality. I am sure the walls echoed the sounds of all our laughter and reached out to her in that moment of reminiscing.

Her eyes turned toward the window where she had stood so many times while washing dishes. She could remember her barefooted little boys running after their father as he plowed the field and then, as they grew older, how they worked so hard beside him. She could almost see the sweat rolling from their brow as the summer heat infused them.

She turned back into the kitchen just in time for another memory to slap her cold in the face: the old phone hanging on the wall. It reminded her of the many times she had waited by it, hoping to hear some news from her son who was in the Vietnam War. A happy memory chased the sad one away as she recalled her three precious little girls watching as she baked cakes, cookies, and pies. She could envision their flour-splattered bodies and the light in their eyes as they licked the icing from the spoon.

As she walked through each room, memories invaded her mind with such force she could scarcely take it all in. She looked into the vanity area, her special place where she had put her makeup on for work and church time and time again. She remembered how she and my father had picked out the yellow tile with such care and excitement, as this was the only home they had ever built together from ground up. She could recall Christmases spent together, ice cream socials, and peanut boiling parties when the first crop of peanuts came in. She could almost hear the old, upright piano playing and the sound of our family singing old hymns together.

With much dread in her heart, she informed my dad of the strange man's visit that day, and of the time frame they had to leave our beloved home and the farm of one hundred acres.

On the farm, they had two large fig trees that produced greatly each year. My mother was saddened to leave these as well because they had been a great source of love across the years as she preserved jar after jar of figs and gave them out to our family, and so many of our friends as well. They wept, both together and separately. They wept...and wept... and wept.

My mother confided in me later, revealing the severe effect this great loss had on my dad's self-esteem as a man. They had lost everything they had poured their lives into. All of the years of hard labor and sweat in the summer heat now seemed in vain.

He and Mom had to find a place to live but since they had no money, they feared homelessness. My dad saw an old, dilapidated house, at least one hundred years old, in downtown Cochran. He went home with joy in his heart to tell my mom about it. He was thankful that he had found a place they could possibly afford, but wanted her to be pleased as well. They drove to the property to look at it together before making a decision. As they walked in the back yard, a peace washed over my mother as her green eyes focused on a huge fig tree: her giving tree. It looked as though there was little left in it, but she felt it was a sign from the Lord of his great provision for this time in their lives.

As she walked through the house, taking everything in, my dad turned to her and asked her what she thought. He must have known what a great disappointment it was, for she was leaving her beautiful, big, brick home with all of its comforts in exchange for something much, much less comfortable. His love for her was so deep; he wanted to provide for her and give her everything her heart desired. After all, she was his queen, or so he had called her for the entirety of their married lives.

She turned to answer him with words that must have brought much healing to his broken heart. Scaling the walls one last time before her green eyes met his, she said, "It is not the house that makes the home, we will make the home."

The old house had belonged to some friends of my parents from years gone by. Only God could have connected the dots of provision. With a heart of generosity and friendship, they rented the old house to my parents for one hundred dollars a month, with the option to buy it when they were more financially stable.

My mother told me much later that she had felt a peace from the Lord assuring her that if she would be faithful, patient, and grateful, then one day He would provide another home for them.

The old house was in need of some love and attention–you could literally see the dirt underneath it through the cracks in the floor. My brother and brother-in-law knew a bit about carpentry and tried to help my parents seal the house enough to make it comfortable in the cold season. Their neighbors expressed concern that they might freeze in the openness of the house but my mother's reply was, "We still have quilts for cover."

Soon the walls were again filled with the laughter of their six children, their spouses, grandchildren, and great-grandchildren, as well as anyone else that needed to be loved. The house smelled like home again with the aroma of coffee, homemade cakes, and fresh cooked vegetables from the garden. Those who came for a visit never left with a sense of emptiness in their spirits or their stomachs. I doubt they even noticed the condition of the old house because they were so welcomed with love and attention. My parents were never too busy to visit with people. They were never too caught up in themselves that they did not take interest in others. I believe that out of this kind of heart for God and others, comes rewards and blessings.

The first year they lived in the old house, their garden produced so many vegetables they were able to fill their freezer and share with the neighbors as well. The corn, cabbage, watermelon, squash, butter beans, peas, potatoes, and okra lined the rows of the garden, a perfect picture proudly displaying the promise of God; the promise that He will provide for us in our greatest time of need. My father tended the ground with a push plow as he had lost all of his mechanically driven farming equipment when he lost the farm. My mother said the fig tree grew so big that year and produced so much fruit that they had to use a ladder to reach the top branches to pick the figs. Mom was so grateful. It was this gift from God that enabled her to give to others. It was truly her giving tree.

After eleven years, the area of town where the house was located was becoming a prime business area. One of my brothers approached my parents with the idea to find a buyer for the place. They were afraid because they felt secure again and did not want to be in debt to anyone ever again. Trusting my brother's good counsel and seeking the advice of a trusted friend, they found that someone was interested in buying the land and the house. The search for another home was on again, only this time under much more pleasant circumstances.

God did it again. Another miracle happened when my parents found another brick home, very much like the one in which I had grown up, for the exact amount of money offered to them for the old house in which they were living. Again they drove to look at the house *together* (as they did everything in life) before making a decision. As they got out of the car, they could not believe their eyes, for there in the back yard was an enormous fig tree. Once again, my mother was given her giving tree as a promise that God was restoring to them what they had lost. She even had a vanity area, her special dressing place. Blessings really do flow to those who are faithful. God says in His word, "This day I have given you both blessings and curses, choose blessings."

My parents could have blamed God. They could have become bitter, and angry, and shook their fist toward heaven in despair. They could have questioned how He could have let something like this happen to people that had served Him faithfully for years with all of their heart, soul, mind, and strength. They could have feverishly reminded God what good people they were, and how they did not deserve everything they had ever worked for in life to be taken from them in their senior years. Instead, they chose to be thankful in every circumstance and to trust that God had it all under control. They praised him regardless of their situation. They continued to reach out to others and to use all that God had blessed them with in order to bless someone else. They did not allow their circumstances to control their actions or rule the day. They acted in love and with a thankful heart for what He had given back to them. They chose blessings and were blessed for it. They were, and still are, true giving trees in my life and in the lives of so many who love them. Their branches reach so high and so wide because they are rooted and grounded in God's love.

They are now in their late seventies and the fruit of their lives is still producing so much that it has to be given away. They are true giving trees. I hope to climb to the top of the ladder someday so that I will be able to reach the entire harvest of their lives in full and become a *giving tree* myself.

THE ELEGANT WOMAN OF GOD MAKES THE BEST OF EVERY SITUATION.

Rather, as servants of God we commend ourselves in every way: in great endurance; in troubles, hardships and distresses; in beatings, imprisonments and riots; in hard work, sleepless nights and hunger; in purity, understanding, patience and kindness; in the Holy Spirit and in sincere love; in truthful speech and in the power of God; with weapons of righteousness in the right hand and in the left; through glory and dishonor, bad report and good report; genuine, yet regarded as impostors; known, yet regarded as unknown; dying, and yet we live on; beaten, and yet not killed; sorrowful, yet always rejoicing; poor, yet making many rich; having nothing, and yet possessing everything.
II Corinthians 6:4-10 (NIV)

ELEGANT REFLECTIONS

In what way were you challenged or inspired after reading the preceding story entitled: *The Giving Trees?*

_____

_____

_____

_____

Reread II Corinthians 6:4-10 (NIV): *Rather, as servants of God we commend ourselves in every way: in great endurance; in troubles, hardships and distresses; in beatings, imprisonments and riots; in hard work, sleepless nights and hunger; in purity, understanding, patience and kindness; in the Holy Spirit and in sincere love; in truthful speech and in the power of God; with weapons of righteousness in the right hand and in the left; through glory and dishonor, bad report and good report; genuine, yet regarded as impostors; known, yet regarded as unknown; dying, and yet we live on; beaten, and yet not killed; sorrowful, yet always rejoicing; poor, yet making many rich; having nothing, and yet possessing everything.*

Do you praise the Lord in every circumstance?

_____

_____

_____

Do you feel challenged by the truth of II Corinthians 6:4-10? Write your thoughts below:

_____

_____

_____

What does it mean to be a 'giving tree?'

_____

_____

_____

_____

Poor, yet making many rich: What do you think this part of today's scripture reference is referring to?

_____

_____

_____

_____

Write in the space below about the things that make you truly rich-I am not referring to money. I want you to dig deep to the things that really matter most in your life:

_____

_____

_____

_____

Prayer: "Father, I am so thankful for my home and family. Thank you also for the gift of good health. Teach me to be satisfied in every situation. I want to respond with elegant godliness to the hardships of life. You are all I need. I trust you to supply. Help me to be a 'giving tree,' even when life is uncertain." Amen.

CHAPTER NINETEEN

THE FENCE

The old house was nestled against the hillside in one of the most scenic settings I had ever seen. Beautiful, large oak trees seemingly stood at attention, as though guarding the property. Lush green grass carpeted the yard from the house to the main road. As I drove past the house every day, I would day dream a bit, wondering about who had originally built the old house and wondering if they were still alive. I imagined a young couple originally built it, perhaps as their forever dream home.

I envisioned them standing hand-in-hand on the heavily wooded lot; pleased they had purchased property so far from the city. The country life was what they had longed for.

Can you see them?

He pulled her gently into his side, eyes gleaming with anticipation as he lovingly whispered in her ear about the children they would raise. She looked deeply into the eyes of the man who had promised her the moon—the one with whom she would share her most intimate moments of life.

The house must be about fifty years old now. I am not sure when it happened, but the city grew through the years and somehow discovered their hidden paradise of dreams. An interstate has been built along the property line. I have a feeling this explains the beautiful, white fence recently installed to encase the property. It makes a clear statement to those who built the interstate, as if it were some sort of billboard announcing: "That's close enough!"

The fence was intended, not for aesthetic purposes, but to establish a boundary. The family paid an enormous amount of money to ensure their private property remains private.

What about you? Have you established healthy boundary lines, letting others know where your *private property lines* begin and end? I am not suggesting we build a fence so high around our lives we end up isolating ourselves from the world. Not at all! A woman of interior elegance reaches in love while sharing with those in need. She opens her heart and home, eagerly offering hospitality. But a woman of interior elegance is wise. She protects those she loves by putting an invisible fence around the precious territories of her life and around the people she holds most dear.

I have heard many women share very private information with other women through the years. I have often cringed, knowing these women were giving away their sacred, private pearls. Giving away the intimate details of your marriage bed is not ok, friend. We must never expose this sacred and intimate gift from God with anyone, other than our husbands. You are his secret keeper and he is to be your secret keeper. Build a strong fence around this area of your life. Build it high and paint it white to represent purity between the two of you.

I have also heard women criticize their spouse and their children in very demeaning ways. I want to encourage you to use good judgment in opening your home for the sake of hospitality, but keep in mind the importance of establishing healthy property lines. Be careful about the conversations you engage in with others while visiting with them. To have one godly woman to share and pray with is different than casting your pearls to anyone within earshot, just to have an audience. Be kind in your conversations concerning your loved ones. If you can't speak edifying things, it is best not to say anything at all! Remember, there are many weak-willed women who would love to whisper sweet words into your husband's ear. I once had a friend who offered to deliver my husband a chocolate cake, while I was out of town. I shared with her once that my husband's favorite dessert was chocolate cake. Being vulnerable and single, she decided to capitalize on this knowledge while I was away, speaking at an event. My husband is a man of integrity and did not accept the offer. I realized I must build a higher fence where this friend was concerned, in order to protect my private property better.

I challenge you to ask the Lord to give you the wisdom needed to protect your private property well. Keep your heart open to serving others. Do not allow the enemy to fill your heart with distrust of ALL people because ONE friend invaded your private property. If you will seek the Lord, He will give you discernment in knowing how to go about establishing your *private property lines.* He will teach you when and where to build a fence in order to protect those you love.

THE ELEGANT WOMAN OF GOD CAREFULLY PROTECTS HER MOST PRECIOUS PEARLS.

Do not give dogs what is sacred; do not throw your pearls to pigs. If you do, they may trample them under their feet, and then turn and tear you to pieces. "
Matthew 7:6 (NIV)

ELEGANT REFLECTIONS

In the preceding chapter, there is connection made between fences and a healthy spiritual life. Were you challenged in any way?

_____

_____

_____

_____

When is it healthy to put a 'fence' around your life?

_____

_____

_____

_____

Reread Matthew 7:6 (NIV): *"Do not give dogs what is sacred; do not throw your pearls to pigs. If you do, they may trample them under their feet, and then turn and tear you to pieces."*

What does it mean to not give dogs what is sacred?

_____

_____

_____

_____

What do you think the scripture means when it tells us to not throw pearls to pigs?

_____

_____

_____

_____

I have experienced sheer embarrassment while over-hearing women share private things that should be kept behind bedroom doors. How is this like casting one's pearl's before pigs?

_____

_____

_____

_____

What, or who, are the 'pearls' in your life?

_____

_____

_____

_____

Prayer: "Father, give me wisdom. Teach me to be discrete. Help me to guard the private, precious 'pearls' in my life, while keeping my heart open to serve others for Your glory."

Amen.

CHAPTER TWENTY

THE OTHER MAN

For privacy purposes, we will call her name Jill. My mother had worked with her for quite some time, and the two women had developed a close friendship. They shared many things together, but my mother had a deep longing to share Jesus with her friend. Since she was by nature a very creative woman, she easily devised an approach that fit Jill's personality. You see, Jill, like many women, loved a good piece of juicy gossip.

One day, while working side by side, Mother said, "Jill, there has been something on my mind that I have needed to share with someone for quite some time now. I just haven't known how to go about it."

Immediately, Jill was a captive audience. "Of course you can tell me anything." Jill responded, "What is it?"

"I am in love with another man."

At this point Jill was in shock, her eyes growing big. "Nadine, do I know this man?"

"I am not sure, you might know him."

"Tell me about him." Jill replied.

"Oh Jill, this man loves me more than my husband ever could, and even though I love my husband greatly and my husband loves me, still he could never do for me what this man does. I can talk to him and tell him anything and he always understands. He is interested in every detail of my life. He cares for my family and my home. Anything I desire, he wants me to come to him. He longs for me to be truly happy. He is the most loving person I have ever met."

Jill's eyes were now about to pop out of her head. She asked, "Does he have any children?"

"Oh, he has lots of kids—I really don't know how many."

With curiosity getting the best of her, Jill asked, "Does your husband know about him?"

"Yes," Mother replied, "and sometimes he visits us and we both talk with him together. My husband knows how I feel about him and he feels the same way about him as well. Even when we are not physically together, it's like I can almost feel his arms of love around me. He loves my children and they love him too."

"What kind of job does he have?"

"Well, he used to be a carpenter. He builds such beautiful things. You have just got to meet him."

Jill was so engrossed in the conversation that she did not even notice when the boss came up to talk with my mother. Then taking notice that he was standing there, Jill asked if she could share with him about this man. "Sure," Mother said. "I don't care who knows about him."

Jill began repeating, almost word for word, everything Mother had shared with her. When she got to the part about the man having been a carpenter, the boss began to smile, his eyes shifting toward my mother, suspiciously. The boss knew Mother to be a woman of God and realized this story must be about Jesus Christ. Her character had been a true testimony and created an influence that demanded respect among her co-workers.

"Jill, I know who Nadine is talking about. He is Jesus!" the boss exclaimed.

Needless to say, Jill was both embarrassed and amazed with my mother's craftiness in sharing with her the character of Jesus, *the other man,* and the deep love my mother had for him.

Jill went home and told her husband about the relationship Mother had with *the other man.* I am sure we would be surprised at how many people have been told this story and how far Mother's testimony has gone.

I have learned a lot from her boldness that day. I now realize that God can give us creative ways to witness to people right where they are, at their deepest point of need. Is there anyone you have been trying to share the love of Jesus with, and yet you feel inadequate to do so?

Oh, my friend, I challenge you to fall head over heels in love with Jesus all over again today. Pray now and ask the Lord to reveal to you a creative way to speak to others about *the other man,* Jesus, and your deep love for him.

THE ELEGANT WOMAN OF GOD FINDS CREATIVE WAYS TO SHARE HER LOVE FOR JESUS WITH OTHERS.

I will fulfill my vows to the Lord in the presence of all his people.
Psalms 116:18 (NIV)

ELEGANT REFLECTIONS

Do you have a favorite store you enjoy shopping at? What a wonderful feeling to find a great deal. Perhaps you have recently discovered a new coffee flavor, or a favorite book? We girls love to share the good news of a great sale, a good recipe, or any other new discovery we have made.

Do you passionately share the good news of Christ with your friends, family, and coworkers?

Write in the space below names of people you care about who do not know our friend, Jesus:

_____

_____

_____

_____

Write down their interest, hobbies, etc.…

Ask the Lord to give you a creative idea to present the good news to them:

_____

_____

_____

_____

Reread Psalms 116:18 (NIV): *"I will fulfill my vows to the Lord in the presence of all his people."*

Have you made a vow to the Lord? What was it? Have you kept it?

_____

_____

_____

_____

A woman of interior elegance wants everyone she knows to meet the savior, Jesus Christ. She willingly shares as God gives opportunity: what He has done and how He has changed the interior of her heart.

How long has it been since you verbally shared what Christ has done for you with others?

_____

_____

_____

_____

Did you see immediate results in their lives or was it a slow progression of changes made over a period of time?

_____

_____

_____

_____

Prayer: "Father, thank you for the good news of the gospel through Jesus, your son. Please give me a courageous heart to share my sweet friend, Jesus, with all whom you desire. Make my heart sensitive and eager." Amen.

CHAPTER TWENTY-ONE

MUSTARD SEED FAITH

Iwas scheduled to leave for Alabama on December 3rd. A friend from my college days had hired me to decorate her new home.

A week or two before I was to leave, I felt deeply impressed that this trip was for a much greater purpose than to decorate a home. I shared this with my husband, Joe, and two very dear friends who I knew would pray for me.

The morning I was to leave, I felt as though I should carry my Bible on board the plane with me. Normally, I would pack it in my briefcase. Although in a rush, I obeyed the still, small voice and carried it in my hand.

My flight was to leave at 1:15 p.m. The destination was Huntsville, Alabama, with a layover in Atlanta, Georgia. I arrived at the airport early, which is quite an accomplishment for me. I love watching people coming and going in such a hurried state. Questions flooded my mind like: where are they going, what kind of life do they lead, are they happy, do they know Christ as their Savior?

My attention was drawn to a gorgeous woman: dark hair pinned up loosely with delicate curls trellising down, eyes blue as the ocean. Her gold silk suit was tailor-made to fit her perfect figure. I watched her talking on her cellular phone. "My, she must have quite a life," I thought. My guess was that she was a successful career woman, had it all together. She was a gorgeous person and could have been a model.

Our flight was announced and boarding began. There we were standing in line, side-by-side. We spoke a casual hello and boarded the plane. Coincidence or God-incidence, our seats were located directly across the aisle from one another. She began our conversation with, "I can't wait to get home to my little boy."

I surprised myself by asking, "What about your husband?"

"I am not married, but I have been living with the same man for three years now. I want to be married but he keeps putting it off. I think I am leaving him when I get back home. He just takes me for granted. We live outside of Atlanta on a twelve-acre ranch. I mow all the grass, feed all the animals, cook, clean, and do his laundry. I do pretty much everything!"

She opened her mouth and a flood of discontentment rushed forth, washing away any preconceived ideas I might have had concerning her *having it all together*. It was obvious she needed to talk.

I told her she was a prize and shouldn't settle for someone who treated her that way.

The seat beside her was empty so I moved over next to her and she continued, "This man is the only father my son has ever known."

She felt guilty about leaving him because of the love her son had for him. I told her children are resilient and that he would be fine in time, that she and her son deserved more. I told her I knew a man who would love her in a way that no one else could. He knows everything about her and loves her anyway. He would be her comfort and strength. He would fill the emptiness she felt. He would even be a father to her fatherless son. Her eyes filled with tears.

"Do you know of whom I am speaking?" I asked.

She told me she had gone to Christian schools while growing up, but her mother had lived another kind of life. She must have sent her daughter to Christian schools in hopes that she would not follow her footsteps. You see, her mother made a career of being a harlot. She said she grew up in hotel rooms, mobile homes, and mansions, all depending upon who her mother's boyfriend was at the time. She had witnessed her mom having an affair with her own best friend's husband for many years. They eventually got married, but the marriage ended in divorce after just two short years.

There was a lot of emphasis on looking good while she was growing up. It made things even more difficult for her now as a young woman. She was twenty-eight years old and had just recently had both breasts removed and reconstructed because of cancer. Her boyfriend hadn't touched her in six months. She felt unloved, unappreciated, and undesirable. She needed a new focus.

We all go through times in our lives when we place too much emphasis on meaningless things. Our need for attention from others often drives us. We all have a God-sized hole in our hearts that only Christ can fill.

In a forty-five minute flight from Raleigh/Durham Airport to Atlanta, Georgia, the woman whom I had sized up as having it all together spilled out her hidden insecurities to a total stranger–Me!

I believe the Lord had that appointment prearranged. He even had kept the seat beside her empty so we could share more intimately. I was in shock. This 'so together woman' was not so together at all. Instead, she was drowning in a sea of loneliness and despair. She needed someone to take notice of her need, someone to throw out a lifeline.

It happens almost daily. We size people up for what we think they are. I am not sure why. Is it out of our own sense of insecurity or simply self-pity? I haven't found the answer yet. I do know that we go through life half asleep, half awake–spiritual zombies. We are not aware of the true needs around us.

Thankfully, I had listened to the Holy Spirit leading me to take my Bible on the plane with me. I led her to Jeremiah 29:11-12. *"For I know the plans I have for you," says the Lord, "plans to prosper you and not to harm you, plans to give you a future and a hope."* Then Proverbs 3:5-6. *"Trust in the Lord with all your heart, lean not on your own understanding, in all your ways acknowledge Him, and He will make your path straight."* We prayed together, asking God to give her strength to do what was right in His eyes. She asked for forgiveness from her sin and strength to make the changes that she needed to make when she returned home.

That day she began a new journey – a journey to discover how to be a woman of interior elegance. She made one powerful decision that set the course of her life on the right path, leading her to discover true beauty that comes only from within; a beauty that is not vain and temporary.

When we parted, I walked away from her in the airport with such an awesome, incredible sense of the Holy Spirit's presence. I wanted to fall on my face and cry, "Holy, Holy is the Lord."

I learned a very valuable lesson that day. People are not what they seem. We are all wrapped in different packaging, but the need inside is the same—the need for a Savior who can take away the darkness and turn all our ugliness into elegance.

I pondered in my heart and mind all that had happened in such a short time. I asked, "Lord, is this what should be happening everyday of our lives? Did this happen because I had such great sense of expectancy that this trip was about more than just making a house beautiful? Did it happen because I had faith to believe, because I was open to your leading? Because I prepared myself by bringing my Bible and because I was alert to the opportunities around me?"

I reviewed the whole scenario, play-by-play. Each time I felt a sense of humility again and again. I asked the same questions repeatedly, "Lord, am I sleepwalking through my life when, in reality, each day you have prearranged appointments with different souls?"

Shame settled in. How many times I must have missed an opportunity to encourage, edify, witness, or to lead someone to Christ. Did I just need to have more faith to believe it could happen?

During my visit in Alabama, I felt a bit preoccupied with all the questions running through my mind, and on the trip home I could not stop thinking about all that had taken place. I found myself looking down at a small charm on my bracelet, a jar of tiny little mustard seeds. I whispered the significant scripture aloud, *"If you have faith of a tiny mustard seed, you can say to this mountain, move from here to there, and it will move. Nothing will be impossible for you."* Matthew 17:20. I repeated it over and over in my mind.

Then the announcement came. It was time to prepare for landing. "Almost back home," I thought. I was excited about sharing with my family all that had happened. I reached to buckle the seat belt and there, in my lap, were scads of tiny little mustard seeds. My first response was sadness for the charm had been a gift from my husband. The golden end cap was missing. I looked at the jar. All the seeds were gone except two wedged down deep in the bottom of the jar. The Holy Spirit immediately spoke to my heart and said, *"You see, it just takes one for you to believe you can be used by me and one for the person who is to receive me as Savior."*

Just before the plane landed, I looked down again. There on the armrest was the gold end cap to my charm. I had not lost anything. Instead, I had gained a new awareness of what God can do in an average day if we have faith to believe. God is awesome! He wastes nothing and will faithfully use us, if we are willing to be broken and spilled out for Him daily.

THE ELEGANT WOMAN OF GOD IS A WOMAN OF FAITH.

If you have faith as small as a mustard seed, you can say to this mountain, move from here to there, and it will move. Nothing will be impossible for you.
Matthew 17:20 (NIV)

ELEGANT REFLECTIONS

Have you ever judged someone wrongly? Write your thoughts in the lines below:

_____

_____

_____

_____

What did you learn from today's story entitled: *Mustard Seed Faith?*

_____

_____

_____

_____

Reread Matthew 17:20 (NIV): *"If you have faith as small as a mustard seed, you can say to this mountain, move from here to there and it will move. Nothing will be impossible for you."*

Share about a time when God amazed you with an opportunity to share His love with someone. Write your thoughts in the space below:

_____

_____

_____

_____

Note: Women often shrink back from women they perceive as prettier or smarter. Intimidation plays a huge part in this avoidance. Intimidation is not from the Lord but from the enemy—the devil. Satan tries to devour any goodness from your life.

Have you ever experienced a time when the person you were avoiding ended up being one of life's greatest blessings?

_____

_____

_____

_____

Can you recall a time in your life when you were disengaged from the world around you? Perhaps you were living inward because painful thoughts were holding you captive. Write about it here:

_____

_____

_____

_____

Think about how small a mustard seed is. Do you have that much faith today? What mountain do you need moved?

_____

_____

_____

_____

Prayer: "Father, give me mustard seed faith. Help me to live my life open to your leading and direction. Help me not to miss out on big blessings because of my big insecurities." Amen.

CHAPTER TWENTY-TWO

KNOWING WHO YOU ARE IN CHRIST

I almost dropped my teeth! I could not believe what I was hearing. The woman sitting just across the dinner table from me continued without taking a breath, "When you were up there speaking last night, I could not believe how much you look like my daughter, especially around the mouth area."

"Oh, how nice," I responded, thinking to myself that since it was her daughter and most moms think the world of their own flesh and blood, it had to be a good compliment.

But then she continued, "Yes, poor thing...had to have so many surgeries."

I sat silent for a moment, not knowing how to reply, and then said, "I am so sad to hear that. What kind of surgery?"

"She had several surgeries on her mouth area."

By this time I was really in shock. I sat listening with what must have been a glazed over sort of look as she continued, "Honey, the poor thing had teeth growing up inside her sinus passages. It took several surgeries to finally correct the problem, but she is the sweetest thing!"

Now girls, when someone says something like that to you, you had better know *who you are in Christ!* I, for sure, did not feel like breaking out into song, *"I feel pretty, oh so pretty, and witty and wise."* I am sure she meant that the spirit within us was similar! Yes, surely she must have meant that!

My two girlfriends began laughing hysterically and could not stop. I began choking on my food because I was laughing so hard and had to leave the table. I still laugh each time I recall that day.

Sometimes there are things said to us by good intending sisters in the Lord and we just have trouble seeing what their purpose is. I am convinced that most of the time, there really is no purpose or intent. We, as women, just enjoy talking. We don't mean it the way it comes out. We just have to give people the benefit of the doubt and somehow find humor in it. If you remember who you are in Christ, it will be a much easier task.

On another occasion, I had a bit of trouble remembering who I was in Christ: the day I attended the funeral of my sister's friend. The family was in the receiving line, standing just in front of the casket. I went up to pay my respect to the deceased lady's sister. Her son, whom I had not seen since we were in high school, was standing next to her. Just as I began to express my condolences, my hand still gently holding hers in sincere sympathy, she turned to her son and said, "Oh, you remember LaTan, don't you honey. I told you she was fifty pounds heavier than the last time you saw her."

They laughed together as I walked away. This hurt me deeply. I cannot deny the fact that I had indeed gained weight. After all, it had been thirteen years since I had seen him and I had just given birth to our third child! But, even though it was true, in this case the truth should have gone unsaid.

If you can remember who you are in Christ when these types of moments present themselves to you, you will be able to handle them in a much more elegant way. Know what you are about. Know that God loves you and that you were bought with a price because He found you to be valuable. Let your confidence come from Him. You are a princess because your Heavenly Father is the King of Kings. You will be able to kick away those ignorant comments. You will be able to laugh, not cover the pain, but unveil the elegant woman of God you really are because you know *who you are in Christ*.

THE ELEGANT WOMAN OF GOD DOES NOT ALLOW MISERABLE PEOPLE TO POISON HER.

Bless those who persecute you, bless and do not curse. Romans 12:14 (NIV)

ELEGANT REFLECTIONS

Why is it important for us to know who we are in Christ?

_____
_____
_____
_____
_____
_____

What is our first instinct when someone offends us?

_____
_____
_____
_____
_____
_____

We want to strike out or cut the person out of our lives altogether. Criticism, even when unintentional can sharpen us if we allow it to. How so?

_____
_____
_____
_____
_____
_____

Reread Romans 12:14 (NIV): "*Bless those who persecute you, bless and do not curse.*"

Why do you think we are to bless those who persecute us?

_____
_____
_____
_____
_____

Has someone spoken something about you that wounded you or made you paranoid?

_____
_____
_____
_____
_____

Giving the benefit of the doubt is the best gift we can give to others and to ourselves. Many times, the person who spoke something that wounded or offended us has no idea! When I think about some of the thoughtless words I have spoken and how my words must have offended or hurt, I realize the importance of giving grace and the benefit of the doubt. Telling yourself: "*They surely didn't mean it that way,*" helps to not hold onto hurt like a warm fuzzy blanket. We must be very careful not to become a victim. We are becoming women of interior elegance and we must hold ourselves to a higher standard. Give the benefit of the doubt. It is the gift that will keep on giving.

Write in the space below a time when someone's words or actions wounded you, even shocked you. Are you done with the pain yet, friend?

_____
_____
_____
_____
_____

While you were writing in the space provided, perhaps you realized you have not surrendered the hurt. If not, let it go, friend! Life is way too short for us to linger over the words of others. Let us linger over the word of God and be healed!

Prayer: "Father, I want to respond the way you would have me respond in each situation of life. Teach me. Guide me. Give me the ability to give the benefit of the doubt to others." Amen.

Chapter Twenty-Three

FROM SMILES TO SCOWLS

She is alone. The bitter scowl on her face makes it obvious that she wants to be left alone. Everyone seems to be a nuisance. With squinted, suspicious eyes and tightly drawn lips, she canvasses the room–critiquing each person with her glaring eyes as she scales them from top to bottom. Her world seems harsh and cold.

I wonder how the old woman came to be this way. I imagine her now foggy eyes once vibrant and alive with hope and a promise of a bright future. She has a smile that in a moment can turn all the lights on in the house. She has incredible joy flooding her entire being and spilling out into the lives of all who come near her. I imagine her filled with compassion as she glances over people and whispers a prayer for each of their souls. She asks God to help her minister to them. She prays for her spiritual eyes to be opened to the needs of others.

That was then – this is now.

I am sure she had no idea it was happening, for she never planned to be a bitter old woman. It happened so gradually. She lost her ability to rise above the situations in her life—those little hurts that often seem so big. They become mountains if not dealt with. Her mind became so consumed with the rude comments others made to her that she could no longer look to the needs around her. She was focused on looking inward, allowing Satan to push the replay button time and time again so she could hear every unkind word that was ever spoken to her. With a tightly clenched jaw, she recalls, over and over again, each bitter memory in slow motion, feeling each as if for the first time, and vowing in her heart not to let anyone mistreat her again.

We must observe her carefully and with no critical spirit. We can learn from her. We must make a decision today to determine in our hearts to not allow life to turn sour for us. We must do a little inventory every day and be intentional about giving over to God each painful event we have faced, for we are the temple of God. We must be careful not to leave His temple a mess: a rubble pile of undone junk. We must lay each painful memory at His feet and keep our heart's door cleared, for living water can only flow freely from a vessel that is open and unblocked.

The old woman can make a change even in this season of her life–so can we. We can choose to be wiser because of the circumstances that have come our way. We have been given a choice to use those painful events as tools of wisdom. Other women can learn from our experiences if we choose to allow God to take control of our lives.

It does not matter what age we are. All of us will face painful events throughout our lives. The only thing that will make us different from the old woman is how we choose to respond to those events. Give God the pain—he will help you to handle everything life deals you, with a positive attitude. De`termine to gain daily wisdom and insight through the power of His word. Don't allow your *smile* to become a *scowl*.

THE ELEGANT WOMAN OF GOD BLESSES OTHERS.

"Bless those who persecute you, bless and do not curse." Romans 12:14 (NIV)

"Create in me a pure heart, O God, and renew a steadfast spirit within me." Psalm 51:10 (NIV)

ELEGANT REFLECTIONS

What did you learn about yourself from the old woman in: *From Smiles to Scowls?* Write your honest thoughts in the space below:

_____

_____

_____

_____

It is so important to consistently do a personal, spiritual, and emotional inventory. Why?

_____

_____

_____

_____

Note: Because life happens, we get caught up in living and responding and often run the risk of becoming bitter without realizing it. In the lines below, write a personal, emotional, and spiritual inventory. Think back to your most carefree days of life. What happened? What events, people, situations changed you? (Good or Bad)

_____

_____

_____

_____

Reread the verses below:

Bless those who persecute you, bless and do not curse. Romans 12:14 (NIV)

Create in me a pure heart, O God, and renew a steadfast spirit within me. Psalm 51:10 (NIV)

How is the Holy Spirit speaking to you?

_____

_____

_____

_____

What situation or relationships have changed you most? Determine to start fresh here in surrender:

_____

_____

_____

_____

Prayer: "Father, you know all things about my life and experiences. Rule over each undone, painful place in my life. Make me aware of your presence and power. Dominate every emotion, every situation, and every old pattern that seeks to destroy me. I love you; I want to radiate your love. Remove the scowl and replace it with a joyful countenance." Amen.

CHAPTER TWENTY-FOUR

FROM HUMILIATION TO HUMOR

I love people. Being around others energizes me. Each week I look forward to being near the body of Christ for worship. On one particular Sunday, I shook hands with everyone in sight, hugging as many friends as possible until I saw my husband drive up under the breezeway of our church to pick me up. My butterfly dance was over now and I went quickly to the car to meet him. I bounced into the passenger seat, still elated with the adrenaline high I always get from being in the presence of my Christian family. My husband glanced over at me, his eyes slowly dropped down to my sweater. Something unusual caught his eye.

With a puzzled look on his face and a chuckle in his voice he asked, "Honey, what in the world is that thing sticking out of your sweater?"

As I looked down toward where he was pointing, the shock of what I saw collided into my horrific embarrassment. About four inches of curved wire was sticking out of my sweater at an upward, slanted curve.

I realized it was the underwire from my miracle bra. It had made its exit through the side of my bra, and then pushed its way further through the knitted sweater I was wearing–for the world to see!

I suppose if anyone would have said something to me about it, I could have saved myself a little embarrassment by saying something like, "Oh, I knitted this sweater myself and since I am not quite finished with it, I left the needle in it to remind me where I left off." But, an untruth would be out of line for a woman striving to become a woman of interior elegance. It would not have been appropriate in God's house for sure!

My husband and I laughed together as the reality of it gripped us both. Our laughter grew and grew as we replayed the scenario: my greeting everyone in the foyer just moments before. I must have looked like the Bionic Woman with a blown fuse since the wire was proudly sticking out inches away from my chest!

I could have stabbed someone when I gave out all those hugs! My imagination ran wild as I envisioned the headline of the morning newspaper, "WOMAN STABS COUNTLESS PEOPLE IN CHURCH FOYER WITH UNDERWIRE FROM HER BRA." I guess I should be thankful that it was a *miracle bra* for it truly was a miracle that no damage was done to anyone physically. I mean, I could have hooked someone as if they were fish bait. What would I have done if I had shish-kabobed someone?

Perhaps you've never had anything embarrassing happen to you. I hope you never experience an embarrassment like mine. But if you do, laughter is the best remedy for a humiliated soul. As we continue to grow into the elegant women we are striving to become, we will be able to laugh at ourselves, knowing these things are no reflection on our intellect. Oh sure, our pride might get a little wounded, but we have opportunity to make life a lot more interesting and fun when we learn to take ourselves less seriously. In doing so, we give others the freedom to laugh at themselves too.

I am so happy my husband and I made a choice to laugh at this humiliating moment in my life and in doing so, we were able to turn our humiliation into humor. What a great guy I married. He loves me in spite of my inelegant moments.

Well, how much more embarrassing can life get? Oh, I am sure I will come up with something.

THE ELEGANT WOMAN OF GOD LAUGHS—A LOT— NO MATTER WHAT!

He will yet fill your mouth with laughter and your lips with shouts of joy.
Job 8:21 (NIV)

ELEGANT REFLECTIONS

Reread the thought for the day: **The elegant woman of God laughs—a lot—no matter what!**

How long has it been since you laughed, really hard?

_____

_____

_____

_____

_____

_____

Reread Job 8:21 (NIV): *"He will yet fill your mouth with laughter and your lips with shouts of joy."*

What encouragement does this scripture verse give you today, given the season of life you are in?

_____

_____

_____

_____

_____

_____

Write down the most embarrassing moment you have ever experienced. Have you been able to laugh and share it with others? If not, why?

_____

_____

_____

_____

_____

_____

Laughter is good medicine. Read Psalm 126:2 (NIV). Write down what you are sad about. Write down a silly thing God allowed that filled your mouth with laughter.

_____

_____

_____

_____

_____

_____

Note: When we take life too seriously and ourselves too seriously, we forget to laugh. God wants to fill us with joy and laughter. The fact that we have been forgiven, bought with His precious blood, and are given opportunities to grow and become women of interior elegance is enough to laugh out loud over!

Do you take life too seriously?

_____

_____

_____

_____

_____

_____

Do you show humor when you are at home or are you too serious and sensitive with your loved ones? Relax. Enjoy your life!

_____

_____

_____

_____

_____

_____

Do you think your family would say that you modeled joy and laughter in your home? If not, start fresh today! It's never too late. After all, we are *BECOMING...*

_____

_____

_____

_____

_____

_____

Note: Freely give the gift of laughter and joy each day. You will be like a breath of fresh air. The world is waiting for your joy. Practice at home.

Prayer: "Father, remind me of the joy I have been given in Christ. Remind me to laugh and enjoy life. Help me to not take myself so seriously. Let pride not hinder my ability to model joy in every circumstance of life." Amen.

CHAPTER TWENTY-FIVE

BEYOND THE WALLS

We must be very careful to not allow the church to become our comfort zone, a place where we escape the world.

Have you ever found yourself going through the motions Sunday after Sunday, sitting on your family-marked pew with an attitude that says: *Bless me if you can?*

Satan finds great pleasure in turning our focus inward instead of outward. He will attempt to make our church family our enemy. His goal is to cause discontentment—finding fault in the pastor or the pastor's wife, how our precious tithe money is spent, what color the carpet should be, etc., that we will not even be aware of what is going on beyond the walls.

Beyond the Walls:

- **Someone is being molested**
- **A woman is being brutally beaten**
- **A teenager is committing suicide**

- A twelve year old is trying drugs for the first time
- A married man is trapped inside the world of pornography
- A betrayed wife, is having an affair with a married man
- A lost girl is filling out an application for a job at the local strip joint
- A drunk is lying in an ambulance fighting for his life
- An entire family has been killed by a drunken driver
- A large number of the teenage population is having sex
- A five year old child has become withdrawn because his mommy and daddy don't want to be married anymore
- A ten year old little boy sits on his front porch, watching a neighborhood gang fight as if it were normal behavior
- An old woman is being mugged
- A single woman is being raped
- Child molesters are preying on children on the Internet and in our communities
- Nursing homes are full of lonely people longing for a visit
- Someone is being kidnapped
- A homeless family is sleeping in the cold of night, huddled together to keep warm

These things are happening, even as we snuggle into our self-appointed church seats—mentally planning our weekly schedules—while the pastor preaches a sermon that we are only half listening to.

The world is waiting for us to make our exit from our comfortable chairs and share the love of Christ. All we must do is look beyond the walls of the church—making ourselves available to the Lord. He will give wisdom—as He faithfully instructs us in the way to go.

He will also give us peace when it is not our appointment. We are not called to minister to everyone, but we are called.

Do you have a willing heart, my friend? A woman of interior elegance is available to God at all times. She is eager to serve Him—eager to be uncomfortable, in order to comfort and show love to His flock.

Your concern for others is living proof that you are truly becoming a woman of interior elegance.

THE ELEGANT WOMAN OF GOD SEEKS TO CHANGE THE WORLD FOR CHRIST.

We are therefore Christ's ambassadors, as though
God were making his appeal through us.
11 Corinthians 5:20 (NIV)

ELEGANT REFLECTIONS

Reflect on this thought a bit longer: Your concern for others is living proof that you are truly becoming a woman of interior elegance.

Ok. It's time to get real. How concerned for others are you?

_____

_____

_____

_____

Reread II Corinthians 5:20 (NIV): *"We are therefore Christ's ambassadors, as though God were making his appeal through us."*

Representing Christ each day is one of the highest honors we are given as believers. Write down examples of how your life reflects an ambassador for Christ?

_____

_____

_____

_____

Note: The elegant woman of God seeks to change the world for Christ.

What are you doing to change the world around you for Christ?

_____

_____

_____

_____

In what ways have you become complacent or comfortable in your walk with the Lord?

_____

_____

_____

_____

How might you influence others to look out the windows of your church to the needs of the world?

_____

_____

_____

_____

Prayer: "Father, I confess I have become complacent in many ways. Forgive me. I desire more of you in my life. Let me not settle for comfortable. Teach me to notice the needs around me and respond as you give resources to do so. Change your church from unhealthy thinking to Godly thinking. Restore us. Renew us. Empower your people, Father." Amen.

CHAPTER TWENTY-SIX

CHRISTIAN

"Mom, can I take an extra snack to school today?" My little kindergarten son asked in a perky voice.

"Sure, honey," I replied, thinking he might be getting hungry before lunch. This went on for about two weeks. I finally asked him if anyone was bullying or bribing him into bring extra snacks to school.

"No Mommy, I am just taking a snack for a little boy in my class. He never has anything to eat during snack time."

My heart sank. "That is very nice of you, Bryce." I said, feeling guilty over the fact that I had thought the worst. "What is the little boy's name?"

"His name is Christian."

Understanding the situation more fully challenged me to buy a few special treats because I wanted to encourage Bryce to be a giver. One week, I bought some Teddy Grahams. Bryce was very excited about them because they were one of his favorite snacks. When he got off the bus in the afternoon, I was waiting for him on the front porch. I watched as he skipped happily down the street, up the drive, and down the walkway to the porch where I greeted him with our usual exchange of hugs and kisses. "How did Christian like his Teddy Grahams?"

"I don't know."

"What do you mean, you don't know. Didn't he seem happy or thank you for them?" I asked, puzzled by his response. Bryce looked at me, his entire face wrinkled into a distorted position.

"Mom, Christian doesn't speak English! We can't even talk to each other!"

My heart melted. I looked down at him tenderly and asked, "Oh Bryce, if you can't communicate with him how did you know he needed a snack?"

His answer to my question transformed my heart forever. With his little face turned upward toward mine, he very innocently said, "I just noticed, Mommy."

I cannot begin to tell you what that moment meant to me. I was absolutely speechless. I sat on the porch swing for quite a long time afterwards. The afternoon sunlight warmed my tear-stained face. "Dear Lord," I prayed, "Please help me to be so in touch with the people you place around me. Help me, Lord, to really notice their need without our needing to say a word to each other, even if we don't speak the same language."

THE ELEGANT WOMAN OF GOD TAKES NOTICE OF THE NEEDS OF OTHERS.

In everything set them an example by doing what is good.
Titus 2:7 (NIV)

ELEGANT REFLECTIONS

Read and reflect on the following statement once again: **The elegant woman of God takes notice of the needs of others.**

How do you take notice of the needs of others?

_____

_____

_____

_____

_____

_____

_____

Reread Titus 2:7 (NIV): *"In everything set them an example, by doing what is good."*

How can we set an example by doing what is good?

_____

_____

_____

_____

_____

_____

_____

NOTE: Today's scripture verse reminds us we are to set an example in EVERYTHING, not just SOME THINGS. This means we must hold ourselves to a higher standard. We are to live our lives noticing those around us and responding appropriately. Consistency is the key to becoming a woman of interior elegance. Loving others well by treating them with respect is of upmost importance.

How were you challenged by the story of Christian and Bryce?

_____

_____

_____

_____

_____

_____

_____

_____

The nations are here in America. With so many cultures coming together in the same cities across the United States, how might we capitalize on this great opportunity to spread the gospel in love to the nations?

_____

_____

_____

_____

_____

_____

_____

_____

Note: Perhaps you can't speak a foreign language. (I struggle also.) I have learned the importance of making direct eye contact. Showing compassion in a smile or gentle gesture is a wonderful way of spreading the gospel to the nations. Love crosses all cultures.

What are your thoughts?

_____

_____

_____

_____

_____

_____

_____

_____

Mother Teresa said it well: "Teach the gospel at all times, and sometimes use words."

How does this challenge you?

_____

_____

_____

_____

_____

_____

_____

_____

Prayer: "Father, I have been self-absorbed and selfish in many ways. I confess I often feel ill-equipped to interact with other cultures as you desire. Give me a spirit of boldness — mingled with love. Make me aware of those who need encouragement. I want to be a giver, not just a taker." Amen.

CHAPTER TWENTY-SEVEN

MOTHER OF THE YEAR

I think I lost my 'Mother of the Year' award today. I forgot to send lunch money to school with my little boy. I did not have socks and underwear washed for my teenage son when he needed them. I forgot to tell my daughter to call her friend back once she had completed her homework. I did not realize the dog needed water in her bowl until the end of the day.

I think my life is much too busy and I am often too preoccupied with trying to take care of the multitude of demands on me as a wife and mother.

You know you have too much on your mind when you open the freezer door to heat up your coffee, or try to put milk in the pantry instead of the refrigerator. Perhaps you can identify with spending an entire afternoon searching the house for your glasses, only to realize they have been on top of your head all along. You know you are too preoccupied when your pencil has been resting behind your ear all day, and you've spent most of the day complaining about the fact that someone always moves your pencil from your desk but never puts it back!

Have you ever spent hours cutting out coupons, yet never remember to take them with you to the grocery store? Or, you write a detailed grocery list with a menu to the side only to leave it hanging on the refrigerator door. Well, these things are really frustrating, but certainly not worth losing the "Mother of the Year" award. We will never be perfect—perfection is only what we strive to achieve. It will only be obtained when we stand before Jesus' throne. Then, and only then, will all the unnecessary pressures of life melt away in a moment, for Jesus makes no unrealistic demands on us—not ever!

We are our *best* and *worst* enemy, convincing ourselves that we have failed somehow if things don't go smoothly in a given day.

So, the next time you are feeling frustrated with your own imperfection and feel you won't be voted 'Mother of the Year,' just remember you don't have to be perfect just yet. Keep trying to do your very best for that is all that is required from you. Tomorrow is a brand new day and you will be back on top of things again. The lunch money will be packed in the book bag, the socks and underwear will be washed, dried, folded, and put away for your son, and you will have written a note to give to your daughter to remind her to call her friend after she completes her homework. The dog will have a full bowl of water early in the day and you will again feel a sense of accomplishment instead of failure.

Always remember that *you* are *still* the 'Mother of the Year' to your own household if you do the best you can *all year*. No matter how bad you goof, no one can replace you!

**THE ELEGANT WOMAN OF GOD KNOWS SHE ISN'T PERFECT
BUT DOES HER BEST IN SPITE OF IT.**

*Trust in the Lord with all your heart and lean not on your own understanding;
in all your ways acknowledge him, and he will make your paths straight.*
Proverbs 3:5-6 (NIV)

ELEGANT REFLECTIONS

Reflect on the following: **The elegant woman of God knows she isn't perfect but does her best in spite of it.**

How does this encourage you in your *becoming a woman of interior elegance* journey?

_____

_____

_____

_____

Reread Proverbs 3:5-6 (NIV): *"Trust in the Lord with all your heart and lean not on your own understanding; in all your ways acknowledge him, and he will make your paths straight."*

How does trusting the Lord with all of your heart change feelings of despair to feelings of hopefulness?

_____

_____

_____

_____

What lies have you believed about your influence as a wife, mother, friend, neighbor, co-worker, etc.?

_____

_____

_____

_____

As you read *Mother of the Year*, what encouraged you?

_____

_____

_____

_____

Note: We must strive to do our best each day. Beware of the voice of defeat. Remember you are the only woman of influence in your home. What an honor. What a privilege. What a joy. How blessed we are to have the Spirit of God with us each day. He is our helper and our friend – the constant One who will not leave us, nor forsake us. Lean hard into His strength today, my friend. He is enough. We don't have to be.

How does this encourage your heart?

_____

_____

_____

_____

Prayer: "Father, thank you for helping me. I want to do my absolute best in all things, for your glory and honor. Teach me to lean hard into your strength and find peace and joy as I serve my family." Amen.

CHAPTER TWENTY-EIGHT

TRUE INNER BEAUTY

The days are lonely. The house is now quiet. Few visitors pass through the doors. Her children, now busy with their own lives, come as often as they can. Loneliness often keeps her company. Her husband of fifty-four years is not the strong protector he once was as Parkinson's disease has taken its toll and fear strikes him suddenly, without any warning. He often cries aloud, a sad, wailing cry that breaks her heart.

Rising with the sun, she prepares his breakfast—making sure he has the proper medication. After bathing him and gently combing his hair, she gives a gentle, supportive hand just behind his elbow as he shuffles across the floor to the kitchen table.

Before the noon hour, many humiliating moments will be shared as these two old lovers realize once again their lives will never be the same. His blue eyes meet hers with a look that says, "I am sorry," as he feels the warm urine he cannot control pour down his clean pants, or as he tries desperately to shuffle to the bathroom before his bowels empty once again with little or no warning. She lovingly cleans him and helps him get into fresh pants, and once again places her tired hand gently into either the small of his back or the bend of his elbow to balance him.

She will make a joke. They will laugh together. Then they will cry as the reality of how their lives have been transformed takes hold of them. It is a bittersweet time in her life as she realizes this is as good as it will ever be.

Sweet memories flood her mind of special days gone by as she sits quietly, reminiscing on the past. She misses the spontaneity of going on a long trip on a moment's notice. She misses feeling his big, strong arms wrapping around her tightly in the night. But her love for this incredible man runs so much deeper than the physical. Her true, inner beauty springs forth each day as she does the most unimaginable tasks in order to make sure he is not humiliated. She is a rare treasure. She died to herself on the day she said, "I do."

She puts the needs of others before her own. She has a quiet strength that rises above even the saddest of days and makes the most of her situation. She is a true, elegant woman of God – My Mother. I hope to be just like her someday when I grow up.

THE ELEGANT WOMAN OF GOD DIES TO HERSELF FOR THE SAKE OF OTHERS.

No one has ever seen God; but if we love each other, God lives in us and his love is made complete in us. 1 John 4:12 (NIV)

ELEGANT REFLECTIONS

Reread the following inspirational quote: **The elegant woman of God dies to herself for the sake of others.**

How do we die to ourselves for the sake of others?

_____

_____

_____

_____

Reread 1 John 4:12 (NIV): *"No one has ever seen God; but if we love each other, God lives in us and his love is made complete in us."*

How does this verse encourage you?

_____

_____

_____

_____

Note: We have no idea what our future holds. Celebrating today with a heart of gratitude is a key component to becoming a woman of interior elegance. Write in the space below your many blessings:

_____

_____

_____

_____

What is the true evidence of God living in someone's heart?

_____

_____

_____

_____

How might you reflect the love of God each day in your own life?

_____

_____

_____

_____

Note: A woman of interior elegance has a spiritual depth about her. She is not shallow. Strength rises up just when she needs it most because she worships the Lord with a thankful heart for today. She does not spend her time wishing for more but is satisfied with all the Lord has blessed her with. Although she doesn't know what tomorrow holds, she does know who holds tomorrow. The love of God strengthens and equips her.

Can you give some examples of how God has strengthened and equipped you?

_____

_____

_____

_____

Prayer: "Father, I worship you. Thank you for your power and strength. Thank you for keeping me strong in the face of hardship. I pray your love will reside in my heart forever. I know you are with me today and will be with me in all of my tomorrows." Amen.

Chapter Twenty-Nine

BE A FRIEND, HAVE A FRIEND

My grandmother told me once: "You have to be a friend, in order to have friends." She was right. But what about the times in life when friends let us down, no matter how good a friend we were to them?

Becoming a woman of interior elegance doesn't happen over-night. It's not a box-mix; just add water and one egg, recipe. It is a journey and each encounter we have with people, both good and bad, help shape us into the women of God we were intended to be. Running away is not the answer. In running away from the conflict, we also run the risk of running away from the growth process.

How do you respond to hurt, or frustrations? How do you react when you've been wounded deeply by someone whom you thought loved you? Do you pout? Shut-down? Have a pity-party? Throw a hissy-fit? Be honest. How do you respond when you feel alone, betrayed, abandoned? Perhaps you have experienced the emotions listed here:

- **You feel used up.**
- **Part of your naivety is gone forever.**
- **You feel misunderstood.**
- **You feel like a fool for having trusted in the first place.**

I have been there, friend. In fact, at some point in time we all have, whether we want to admit it or not. Your thoughts get scrambled trying to figure some things out, but there are some things you will never be able to figure out. It is then you best let it go!

A woman of interior elegance disciplines her emotions. She determines in her heart not to be shaken by the wrong doings of others. Get up, girlfriend! Get up! You might feel like you will never be able to be the fun-loving, happy-go-lucky person you once were. You might not be her again. But I can tell you, with Christ on your side, you will be better than your old self. The world will have to take a step back at the newly revised version of you-elegant woman!

I want to challenge you to change your perspective from worrying about having right friendships, to being the right friend. Let's determine in our hearts to use wisdom in friendships. We can be friendly with everyone but we are not to be best friends to all. I am amazed by the stories of women who are hurt by their girlfriends, but they keep going back for more of the same bad behavior. Meanwhile, there is a sweet, godly woman waiting in the wings of their lives who would be true-blue. When we are healed up from the inside out, God will begin to draw us to healthy people.

What kind of friends are you hanging with? Careful now, we become like those we spend the bulk of our time with.

A True Friend:

- **Loves you for who you are.**
- **Celebrates your God-given gifts, talents, and abilities.**
- **Spurs you on toward good deeds.**

- **Celebrates your victories.**
- **Is deeply saddened to see you fall.**
- **Is available to listen.**
- **Cares about all that interests you as a person, even if it doesn't interest her.**
- **Is excited to see you win.**
- **Is never jealous or competitive.**
- **Seeks the beauty you cannot see in yourself.**
- **Defends you when others criticize you.**
- **Speak gentle truths—drawing you back to God's reality.**
- **Does not fertilize ungodly thoughts and feelings.**
- **Drives you toward spiritual elegance and away from ugly gossip.**
- **Knows you are not perfect and yet, loves you in spite of it.**

My dear friend, Sandy, reminds me often that God wastes nothing. A woman of interior elegance puts on her big-girl panties and gets on with life. She doesn't allow others to cripple her, or hold her back from her purpose. She acknowledges everything as a learning experience. After all, the most unpleasant circumstances in life hold incredible power to refine and shape a person into God's image. A woman of interior elegance wisely discerns that human hardship is heavenly hardware from God's perspective. He will use hardship as tools to reshape our thinking, strengthen us, and help us.

The best training we can receive on friendship is rejection. I feel I have learned to be a much better friend for having gone through painful betrayals. Jesus was betrayed on every level and yet, His character and commitment to us stood strong. He was not defined by the pain of rejection but by His victory on the cross.

By what is your life defined? Have you allowed the pain of rejection to defeat you in every aspect of life? Today is a new day, my friend. Mark it on your calendar in bold print: **FRESH START.**

THE ELEGANT WOMAN OF GOD IS MORE CONCERNED WITH BEING A FRIEND, THAN HAVING FRIENDS.

A friend loves at all times. Proverbs 17:17 (NIV)

Therefore, if anyone is in Christ, he is a new creation;
the old has gone, the new has come
II Corinthians 5:17 (NIV)

ELEGANT REFLECTIONS

Reread 11 Corinthians 5:17 (NIV): *Therefore, if anyone is in Christ, he is a new creation; the old has gone, the new has come.*

What hope does this give you? How can we become a new creation?

_____
_____
_____
_____
_____
_____

Do you feel you are a good and trustworthy friend? What qualities make you a good friend?

_____
_____
_____
_____
_____
_____

How do you determine who is a good and trustworthy friend?

_____
_____
_____
_____
_____
_____

When you look back over the course of your life, do you see spiritual growth and maturity in the way you approach friendship?

_____

_____

_____

_____

_____

_____

How is human hardship heavenly hardware?

_____

_____

_____

_____

_____

How can hardships reshape our thinking?

_____

_____

_____

_____

_____

Why is it important to steer away from gossip, even among best friends? Read Proverbs 16:28 (NIV).

_____

_____

_____

_____

_____

How does gossip separate close friends?

_____
_____
_____
_____
_____
_____

Read Proverbs 11:13 (NIV): *A gossip betrays a confidence, but a trustworthy person keeps a secret.* Write your thoughts about this below:

_____
_____
_____
_____
_____
_____

Prayer: "Father, teach me to be a good and trustworthy friend. Help me be a person of godly integrity—a woman of interior elegance." Amen.

CHAPTER THIRTY

SETTING THE MOOD OF YOUR HOME

As women, you and I have been given many special blessings. One of the most important blessings we have been given is the blessing of setting the mood of our home. Within you and me lives a power to create beautiful things because we're made in the image of the master of creation.

Home is where we let our guard down and get *real* with ourselves. It is the one place we can fully relax and let go. After all, no one is looking—right? Oh no, my friend! All eyes are on us. We are the queen of our palace. If you are reading this book, chances are you are ready for change. Chances are you wouldn't be reading a book entitled: *Becoming a Woman of Interior Elegance,* unless you desire to *become* a woman of interior elegance. So, let's get real with ourselves and with God.

Ask yourself these questions:

- **What kind of mood do I set for my family?**
- **Am I pleasant while out in the world but the 'witch of the west' once at home?**
- **Do my mood-swings cause my family to walk on eggshells?**
- **Am I hot-tempered and out-of-control?**
- **Am I seeking new ways to exemplify Christ's power in my home, or trying to get my own way?**
- **Do I use my words well?**
- **Do I refresh others, or drain them emotionally dry?**

Everyone has a bad day from time to time. A bad day can be mood-altering. But as women of interior elegance, we must practice self-control. Our mood-swings can be unpredictable and ungodly. A bad mood affects others, and can become a cancer that attacks anyone who comes near us. We affect those around us either in a positive or negative light. The choice is up to us.

Home is the expression of who we really are. It can become our offering of praise for all God has blessed us with. As we pour our hearts into every detail, whether cleaning, decorating, or setting the mood in our attitude and actions, we will begin to reap a harvest of blessings as true obedience flows from our grateful hearts. In that, we are able to consciously make our home a better, healthier, emotionally secure environment for our families and friends. It all depends on our own temperature gage.

Just before my wedding day, a dear, elderly lady of God gave me a good piece of advice by saying, "You will be the one to set the mood of your home, La-Tan." That statement made a deep impression in my mind and has influenced how I respond to my family and friends.

I learned quickly how true that statement is. There have been many days when I did not set a peaceful mood for the rest of my household. Before I knew it, the entire family was snapping at one another. Then, on other more conscious days, I have made a real effort to light a candle and perhaps play some soft music to relax myself before the troops come home. What a difference it makes! A candle often seems to send a calming effect across my spirit and before I realize it, I am able to put things in perspective and not take my frustrations out on anyone else. Well, maybe this will require lighting a candle *and* saying a prayer or two! My point is: there is never any excuse for setting 'Sister Ugly' loose! God's word tells us that we are able to take every thought captive. It is not an easy task! Nevertheless, it is important that we keep in mind the incredible gift it is to be able to encourage and give light and life to our families.

Our actions say a lot about exactly what is going on inside of us. We don't even have to open our mouths or speak a word, for what is on the inside will come out whether we want it to or not. We must be ever aware of the kinds of things we are listening to during the day. We must be very sure not to allow other people to pour poison onto us by listening to bitter conversations too often. As soon as someone rubs us the wrong way, we will rub that same poison onto someone else. Make sure you have more balcony friends than basement friends. If you choose the reverse, I fear you will live your life in the basement and the walls will be lined with bottles of poison.

I pray we will be ever so focused that we grow in our walk with the Father. I pray we will be determined to make a goal of filling our minds with good, positive, edifying things because whatever goes in comes out. We need to practice acting the part of the woman in Christ that we would want our children to remember us as.

What mood do you long to set for your family? Practice, practice, and practice some more for practice makes perfect!

THE ELEGANT WOMAN OF GOD REFRESHES OTHERS.

A generous woman will prosper; she who refreshes others will herself be refreshed.
Proverbs 11:25 (NIV)

ELEGANT REFLECTIONS

Reread the following statement: The elegant woman of God refreshes others.

Think about how you might refresh others. Write your thoughts in the space below:

_____
_____
_____
_____

Reread the scripture verse: *A generous woman will prosper; she who refreshes others will herself be refreshed.* Proverbs 11:25 (NIV)

How does this verse challenge you?

_____
_____
_____
_____

What kind of mood do you set within your home?

_____
_____
_____
_____

Are you consistent, or do you struggle with moodiness?

_____
_____
_____
_____

Have you ever had a bad day that put you in a really bad mood? How did your bad mood affect everyone else in your family?

_____

_____

_____

_____

Note: As we strive to become women of interior elegance, it is important to allow the Holy Spirit dominion over our emotions and moods. We want our families to look forward to spending time with us, not dread it. Write in the space below how the Lord is dealing with you concerning this:

_____

_____

_____

_____

A woman of interior elegance works hard to be consistently kind. Her emotions do not dominate her mood, or the way she treats her family. Are you consistently kind?

_____

_____

_____

_____

Prayer: "Father, help me set the mood of my home in a way that is pleasing to You. Teach me how to be gentle and kind, consistently." Amen.

CHAPTER THIRTY-ONE

ELEGANT WARRIOR

W hat kind of woman delivers a cupcake, adorned with a beautifully lit candle, to the chemotherapy ward in order to celebrate another's last day of treatment—when she herself, had chemo treatments to complete? I'll tell you what kind of woman—a woman of interior elegance, my late mother-in-law, Mrs. Betty Duncan Murphy.

She courageously battled cancer for fourteen years. The cancer originated in the colon before spreading to the lymph nodes and liver. It had reoccurred in the lung six times, but she fought even harder to live. According to statistics, she should have died a year and a half after the original diagnosis. But God doesn't deal with statistics. His mighty, healing hand kept her alive, time and time again.

She was a fighter and a true inspiration to me, and to all who had the blessing of knowing her. Even as death stared her down, she exemplified incredible, supernatural determination to live. And live she did. Interior elegance spilled out to those around her. She was selfless and giving, even on her weakest days—intent on writing letters of encouragement, and making meals for anyone who needed extra love and attention.

A mutual friend of ours once shared with me how Mrs. Betty ministered to her. While out of town on vacation in the small town where my mother-in-law lived, our mutual friend ended up in the hospital with a blood clot. She told how discouraging it was to be away from her home, in a strange hospital, with no family nearby.

A knock came at her door. Slowly the door began to open, revealing an angel of mercy standing there before her eyes, my mother-in-law— an elegant woman of God. She had just completed another round of chemotherapy but even that didn't keep her from coming to visit her friend. She was thin and pale, her balding head wrapped neatly in a turbine. With a beautiful bouquet of flowers in hand and a consoling smile across her hollow, beautiful face, she brought comfort and cheer to a frightened, lonely sister. She represented the true picture of a godly elegant woman.

My friend said she would never forget that day because she realized how much she had to be thankful for. The Lord had sent her an angel, an angel that had learned how to truly die to herself—looking to the needs of others regardless of her own problems.

Would you be able to think of someone else's need even as you faced chemotherapy and the uncertainty of your own life?

THE ELEGANT WOMAN OF GOD TENDS TO THE NEEDS OF OTHERS.

Give and it will be given to you. A good measure, pressed down, shaken together and running over, will be poured into your lap. For with the measure you use; it will be measured to you. Luke 6:38 (NIV)

ELEGANT REFLECTIONS

Reread Luke 6:38 (NIV): *Give and it will be given to you. A good measure, pressed down, shaken together and running over, will be poured into your lap. For with the measure you use; it will be measured to you.*

How does this verse challenge you?

_____
_____
_____
_____

When was the last time you served someone else in his or her time of need?

_____
_____
_____
_____

After reading the story entitled: *Elegant Warrior*, what might you need to do differently in your life each day?

_____
_____
_____
_____

What is it that makes a woman elegant?

_____
_____
_____
_____

Reread today's inspirational thought: **The elegant woman of God tends to the needs of others.**

How do you tend to the needs of others?

_____

_____

_____

_____

Look in the back of your Bible concordance. How many scripture references do you find on serving? (Also look for servant, service, served, servant.)

_____

_____

_____

_____

Prayer: "Father, I confess I have been self-absorbed. Forgive me, Lord. Help me to live a life of service that is pleasing to you. Teach me your ways and help me to walk in them." Amen.

CHAPTER THIRTY-TWO

MIRACLE AT THE GATE

Rejection and loneliness gripped me like a vice. Moving to a new town and leaving behind close friends can leave a deep, empty void in one's heart. My husband and I had been married ten years and had moved six times during that short time span. To top that off, we had just moved into what I thought was my dream home: the one we would raise our children in, the one in which we would grow old together. I had barely unpacked the last box when the shocking news came that we would be moving—for the seventh time. This time, we would be moving out of state. It was a wonderful job promotion for my husband, and one he simply could not refuse.

I had given birth just three weeks before. My emotions were running rampant.

After the move I would often ask myself, "What is wrong with me? Why can't I snap-out of this whiney-hinny-mode and be happy here?"

Wrestling with loneliness can be exhausting. The true challenge was that our house was only one of three completed in our new subdivision, so I had no neighbors with whom to make friends. After attending church a few weeks, I called a lady to see if she would be interested in having lunch together. She told me her plate was full and that she really did not have time for any new friendships in her life—then proceeded to tell me about another lady who might be in need of friendship. Rejection and loneliness attacked with full force.

It was not in my nature to live in a *pity-party* state of mind. I was sick and tired of it. With renewed determination, I told the children that we would no longer sit around, wishing we could return to our old home. Instead, we would do something tangible to help others who might be experiencing the same feelings of transitional loneliness. We began baking homemade cookies by the dozen. Each time a new family moved in, we would deliver a fresh dozen of piping-hot, chocolate-chip-cookies.

I also decided, rather than waiting to be invited, I would be the one to do the inviting to my home. One day, I invited a lady and her three children to go swimming at our neighborhood pool. She was to bring sandwiches for her family and I prepared four peanut butter sandwiches for our three children and myself. While sitting around the pool, chatting and watching the children swim, I realized she had not brought lunch. How embarrassed I was! I must have misunderstood.

"Not a great first impression." I thought. I whispered a prayer, "Lord, please multiply this food today."

Stalling for time, I walked over to say hello to the lady working as gatekeeper of the pool. I quickly told her about how I had misunderstood, thinking my friend was bringing lunch for her children and how embarrassed I was to have misunderstood. I jokingly asked her to pray that the Lord would multiply our peanut butter sandwiches like he multiplied the fish and the bread in scripture.

I walked over to the table where my guest and her three children were waiting. I slowly began passing out the four sandwiches I had brought— explaining all the while how sorry I was that I didn't bring more. There were eight of us. Four sandwiches was definitely not enough food for six hungry little swimmers and two hungry adults. She was very kind and forgiving, assuring me it was okay.

Suddenly, a voice called out to me from across the pool, "La-Tan, come here, you won't believe this!"

As I walked over to my friend, the gatekeeper, I could not believe my eyes. My miracle had come in the form of a pizza delivery boy! My friend began to explain that he came to the gate and told her his employer was giving away free pizza that day. She could not believe it, either. She began telling me how strange that was and that it had never happened before. She had never even heard of such a thing. With a huge grin spread across her sunburned face, she handed me two very large, piping hot pizzas and said, "Wow, your prayers really did get answered."

The Lord really does take care of His people: sometimes in big ways and sometimes in the more simple things of life. He is tender and genuine—concerned about all that concerns us. He reminded me, that day, that I was not alone. He was there. He meets us at our point of need and honors our attempt to be faithful to him, in ways we cannot begin to imagine.

Peace washed over my heart and soul with the realization that the Lord would provide all of my needs, even in this strange city. He had provided lunch that day and he would soon provide precious, new friendships. I felt an assurance that everything would be all right and in time, I would feel very much at home in this now unfamiliar place.

I learned a big lesson that day. We do not have to wiggle restlessly in the palm of God's hand while trying to force Him to move the way we want Him to move. He is in control of every situation. There is nothing that enters into our lives that he has not sifted through His mighty hands first. He is faithful to provide for all of our needs—even the most basic needs.

If you are in a vulnerable situation, if you feel your world has been turned upside down, if you fear you will never feel the same again—don't panic! Look up my friend, just across the way, to where the gatekeeper stands. You just might find the answer to your prayers waiting for you there—a true *miracle at the gate!*

𝔇

THE ELEGANT WOMAN OF GOD BELIEVES.

What is impossible with men is possible with God
Luke 18:27 (NIV)

ELEGANT REFLECTIONS

Reread Luke 18:27 (NIV): *What is impossible with men is possible with God.*
Luke 18:27 (NIV)

Write in the space below about how God did the impossible for you and
your family.

_____
_____
_____
_____

Have you ever experienced loneliness? How did you move beyond your
feelings?

_____
_____
_____
_____

Have you ever moved to a new place and had difficulty making friends?

_____
_____
_____
_____

Share how the story entitled: *Miracle at the Gate,* ministered to you.

_____
_____
_____
_____

Note: The elegant woman of God chooses NOT to have a pity-party.

Why is it important to NOT linger in pity-parties?

_____

_____

_____

_____

By making the choice to be "others-minded," we are giving ourselves the best gift we could ever imagine. How can this be?

_____

_____

_____

_____

Prayer: "Father, teach me to look beyond myself, my loneliness, and my pain. Help me to be as others-minded as possible. Develop godly character in my life that resists pity-parties." Amen.

CHAPTER THIRTY-THREE

THE FOCAL POINT

Leonardo de Vinci painted a beautiful piece of art, like no other. The infamous painting I am referring to is, *The Last Supper.*

The Last Supper depicts Jesus dining for the last time with his closest friends, his disciples. As an artist, Leonardo realized that our eye is drawn to the center of a painting, to whatever the focal point is, and how important it was for him to have a center of interest in his art. There is incredible power in the center focal point. Without it, the painting would have little or no power to move the viewer's heart. In this particular piece of work, Leonardo painted Jesus at the center. He did not paint Jesus to either side or at the end of the table, but in the center.

I have given the idea of the *power of the center focal point* quite a bit of thought. I found myself wondering: *If this famous painting represented my life, where would Jesus be painted in? Would He be the focal point of my life, or would He be some place off to the side—giving the power of the focal point to someone or something else? Would he be the place all eyes would be drawn to? Would they recognize that because He was painted at the center, my life had new meaning? Would they realize that just by His being there, everything else made sense?*

My friend, you and I must stay focused on allowing Christ to remain the focal point of our lives or perhaps He will be painted underneath the table, hidden so as not to offend anyone. Other things in our lives will begin to take the center position—our jobs, friends, neighbors, church, responsibilities, or our need to impress others. We must not allow anything or anyone to take center-stage of our life canvas. If we are to become women of interior elegance, Jesus is not to be hidden—out of sight and out of mind.

Without Christ at the center, our lives will be out-of-balance. Our priorities will become skewed. His power is the grounding force lighting all dark, dreary places in our lives.

Where is Jesus painted on the canvas of your life, today? Focus, my friend, focus on the center of our hope and joy– *the power of the center focal point—Jesus*!

THE ELEGANT WOMAN OF GOD HAS CHRIST AS HER FOCAL POINT.

Let us fix our eyes on Jesus, the author and perfecter of our faith, who for the joy set before him endured the cross, scorning its shame, and sat down at the right hand of the throne of God. Hebrews 12:2 (NIV)

ELEGANT REFLECTIONS

Reread today's inspirational thought: **The elegant woman of God has Christ as her focal point.**

How does Christ's power keep your life balanced?

_____
_____
_____
_____
_____
_____

How was your life out-of-balance before Christ?

_____
_____
_____
_____
_____

Reread Hebrews 12:2 (NIV): *Let us fix our eyes on Jesus, the author and perfecter of our faith, who for the joy set before him endured the cross, scorning its shame, and sat down at the right hand of the throne of God.*

Why it is important for us to fix our eyes on Jesus?

_____
_____
_____
_____
_____

After reading today's story entitled: *The Focal Point,* how were you challenged?

_____

_____

_____

_____

_____

_____

Write a list of things that war against Christ being your center of focal point?

_____

_____

_____

_____

_____

_____

If your life were a painting, where would Jesus be positioned?

_____

_____

_____

_____

_____

_____

How does keeping Jesus at the center of your life help you remain strong each day?

_____

_____

_____

_____

_____

_____

Think about the times in your life when Jesus was not at the center. How was your life different then?

_____

_____

_____

_____

_____

_____

Prayer: "Father, I invite you to be the center of my life. You are the center of my hope and joy. Forgive me for the times I have painted you into the corner of my life. Please remain my center of focal point forever." Amen.

CHAPTER THIRTY-FOUR

GOD IS GOOD

Bright-red nail polish was splattered generously over the cream col-ored carpet. My eyes followed the red path leading from the closet door, opening to tiny Fred Flintstone feet, all the way up to the top of his three-year-old kneecaps. I could not believe my eyes.

Just moments before I had been searching for him, going from room to room calling, "Bryce, where are you?" But no answer came. There was only one last place to look—the master bedroom closet. There he was, dressed in nothing but his diaper. His chubby legs were painted from the knees down. (I must say, he did a pretty good job of polishing his toenails).

"Oh Bryce," I said in despair—realizing the memory of this moment would be forever embedded into the cream colored carpet.

I stood looking down at his precious round face, his curly blond hair highlighted by the sunlight coming through the window behind him. He wrinkled his tiny nose and snorted a little laugh as he looked up at me and said, "Isn't God good, Mamma?"

I could not hold back the laughter. I was amazed he could think of such a clever comment at only three years of age. He was old enough to realize he was in big trouble, and desperate to divert my attention away from the mess he had made.

"Yes, Bryce, God certainly is good, because only God himself could save you from the spanking you deserve."

I still chuckle each time I remember that day.

Later, I wondered if I too, acknowledge the goodness of God only when I find myself in the middle of some big mess I have made. Is He a God of convenience, or do I give Him the continual recognition He so deserves?

My friend, are you hiding the messes you have created in the closet of your life? Do you hear the Father calling you— *"My daughter, where are you?"*

Even though He knows exactly where you are, He still loves you enough to give you a choice. Are you willing to be found by Him, or are you still hiding there in your private sin? Are you willing to confess it, or are you feverishly attempting to divert His attention away from the real problem onto something else?

He will shine His great light on the mess you have created and wipe it away in a moment, if you will just stop hiding. Once you answer His call, He will wipe away every stain that has kept you in your secret place and childish guilt. No memory of it will be embedded permanently anywhere in His memory.

He loves you! He loves you! Isn't God good? He is so very, very good!

THE ELEGANT WOMAN OF GOD NEVER HIDES FROM GOD.

For there is nothing hidden, that will not be disclosed, and nothing concealed, that will not be known or brought out into the open. Luke 8:17 (NIV)

ELEGANT REFLECTIONS

Reread the inspirational thought for the day? **The elegant woman of God never hides from God.**

Are you hiding anything from God?

_____
_____
_____
_____

Reread Luke 8:17 (NIV): *For there is nothing hidden, that will not be disclosed, and nothing concealed, that will not be known or brought out into the open.* Luke 8:17 (NIV)

What are your thoughts concerning the scripture verse?

_____
_____
_____
_____

After reading today's story entitled: *God is Good,* write how you were inspired or challenged?

_____
_____
_____
_____

Can you think of a time in your life when you knew to do right but chose to do wrong anyway?

_____
_____
_____
_____

Instead of confessing your sin to God right away, did you try to divert His attention to something else in your life?

_____

_____

_____

_____

How does sin make you feel after the fact?

_____

_____

_____

_____

If there are any hidden sins in your life, confess each one on the lines below—exposing each one in the full light of God.

_____

_____

_____

_____

Prayer: "Father, I confess each hidden sin today. Expose, purify, and cleanse me fully so that I can be free. Wash me so that I can be whiter than snow in your sight, free of every sinful stain." Amen.

CHAPTER THIRTY-FIVE

DEFENDING OTHERS

My first experience with hanging wallpaper was when we lived in South Carolina. It was a floral pattern with tiny peach and green accents—very Victorian in style. I was so proud of myself. I stood back after completing the job to take another look. The feeling of accomplishment made the hard work worth it.

That was before the birthday party—the party my daughter would be given the supposedly washable magic markers.

Days later, the kids were unusually quiet. *Where are they?* I wondered, while searching room-by-room. At last, I found them in my newly wall-papered bedroom. I could not believe my eyes. They were still in action, tiny arms moving quickly in circular motion, drawing murals all over the wallpaper. The shades of purple, green, and blue had penetrated and bled through into the bottom layer of the paper. 'Washable only on hard surfaces' is how the box of so-called washable markers should have read.

They both began to cry when they saw the look on my face, a dead give-away that they understood what they were doing was wrong. I was so upset. In fact, I am not sure they had ever seen me so angry.

Kyle began to plead their case immediately, *"Mommy, wook at da' purty rainbow 'Nae drew—don't pank her Mommy."*

His love for his sister came through loud and clear, as he defended her. He did not want his little sister to get into trouble. He was thinking of her more than himself, for he had been just as involved as she had.

That day left me with something to consider about the way I deal with others. I had to ask myself, "Am I quick to come to the defense of others, or quick to point a finger to blame?"

As women of interior elegance, we will continue to strive toward godly character each day. Let us be quick to defend and protect. I pray we will always be considerate of those we love, even to the point of placing their best interest above our own. Let us be slow to point out the mistakes others have made and quick to point out the good things they have accomplished. I pray we will seek out beauty in others, as if it were a beautiful rainbow drawn on the canvas of our lives.

THE ELEGANT WOMAN OF GOD SEEKS TO FIND GOOD IN OTHERS.

Whatever is true, whatever is noble, whatever is right, whatever is pure, whatever is lovely, whatever is admirable – if anything is excellent or praiseworthy – think about such things. Philippians 4:8 (NIV)

ELEGANT REFLECTIONS

Reread the inspirational thought for today: **The elegant woman of God seeks to find good in others.**

Do you look for the good in others, or do you look for faults?

_____

_____

_____

_____

Reread Philippians 4:8 (NIV): *Whatever is true, whatever is noble, whatever is right, whatever is pure, whatever is lovely, whatever is admirable – if anything is excellent or praiseworthy – think about such things.*

In order to become a woman of interior elegance, what must change?

_____

_____

_____

_____

Do you focus on whatever is pure, lovely and admirable?

_____

_____

_____

_____

Is it acceptable for us to think critically about others?

_____

_____

_____

_____

Does thinking critically about others feed our own ego?

_____

_____

_____

_____

Do you defend others well? When should we defend others?

_____

_____

_____

_____

Read Psalm 51:7 (NIV): *Cleanse me with hyssop, and I shall be clean, wash me, and I shall be whiter than snow.*

Note: In today's story, my children had made a big mess on the wall. I was unable to wash the mess away. When we mess-up, or sin, Jesus washes us whiter than snow—as soon as we repent and confess Him as Lord. If you have not asked Christ to forgive you of your sins, do it now in the space below. You don't need to use fancy words. Be yourself. Speak to Him from your heart. Perhaps you are a believer but have made a mess on the wall of your life. All of your efforts to wash the mess away have been in vain. Ask Christ to cleanse, purify, and renew your soul. Rededicate yourself to him on the lines below:

_____

_____

_____

_____

Prayer: *"Father, cleanse my heart. Wash away every sin. I confess each one to you now. Make my heart whiter than snow." Amen.*

CHAPTER THIRTY-SIX

GOOD ENOUGH

A s I stood in the middle of the airport terminal among hundreds of people, with my arms stretched high above my head and my legs spread widely apart, I felt totally humiliated. I could not believe I was being made such a spectacle. The security guard waved the scanning devise up and down places on my body that I don't want to mention, while everyone who was in the line behind me, looked on.

It was only three weeks after the September 11th horror when the Twin Towers went down, and all of America went into panic-mode after realizing our country had lost many precious lives to the hands of terrorists. *Freedom* would never again have the same meaning.

I was to be in Chicago that night to speak at an event; circumstances leading up to this moment had been less than pleasant. The airline failed to inform me of my flight cancellation. I would be switched to another flight that was leaving in ten minutes. Ten minutes! My nerves were absolutely shot. This was the first time I had flown since the attack on the United States. That alone would have been stressful enough, but now I was forced to run through the airport dragging my luggage behind me-very heavy luggage may I add. I did not have *proper ticketing* because of the airline's mistake. As a result, I had been randomly entered into the computer system as *suspicious.*

There I stood, stretched out in front of God and everyone, while the security guard proceeded to dump the contents of my carry-on luggage and purse onto the security counter. I watched in total disbelief

The security guard began rummaging through my personal belongings, asking if I had any sharp objects in my possession. By this point, I was totally annoyed and responded a bit sarcastically, "Yes, as a matter of fact, that right there is a very sharp object." The guard turned toward me, stunned by my bold comment. "Yes," I continued, in a tone of voice that might have said: *I will use this opportunity to tell him about Christ or bust!* Pressed for time, I began speaking in turbo speed. "That is the word of God. It is sharper than any two edged sword."

The tension that had been in his face softened into a partial smile.

"You are a Christian, aren't you?"

"Yes, I am as a matter of fact. Are you?"

"Probably not as good of one as you are."

"Well, I don't know about that. None of us can ever be *good enough.*" As I pointed down at my belongings, I said, "There is nothing in that book that says anything about our having to be good enough."

I began to speak faster as I realized the plane was almost completely boarded and I, for sure, did not want to miss my flight.

"The only requirements that I know about are these: Do you believe that Jesus is the Son of Man; that He was born of a virgin mother, Mary; and that He came into this world for the purpose of dying on a cross so that you might be forgiven of your sins and have eternal life in Him? Do you believe these things?"

"Yes," he said nodding his head. He smiled as he placed the last of my speaking material, Bible, and other belongings back into my carry-on luggage. "I was taught all of those things, when I was a boy."

"Do you believe in them now?"

"Yes I do!"

"Well then sir, guess what? You have just won a free ticket into heaven. The scriptures say that, *if you confess me before men, I will confess you before my Father in heaven.*"—Matthew 10:32 (NIV)

He smiled a big smile and said, "God bless you, ma'am."

As I walked away, I felt so blessed to have had that opportunity. As frustrating as it was, God had a plan in mind. It wasn't about *me* at all!

As I have told you many times throughout the pages of this book, I have not always been obedient in seeking out ways, or allowing God to use me for His good. However, I do know that, without a doubt, He longs for us to be ever-ready to be used by Him on a daily basis. It is possible in both big and small ways.

There is urgency now more than ever before. The time is drawing closer and closer as scripture is being fulfilled. Christ will return, just as He said He would. The world is hungry to know Him as Lord.

Today, there is someone who needs to be reminded that it is not about being *good enough*. The gift of his love and forgiveness is free to all who will confess Him as Lord of their life.

Do you believe? Have you asked Him into your heart? Are you eager to confess Him, unashamedly, to others? He will claim you as His own when you pass from this world into heaven. Then you will stand before the throne of God and Jesus might say something like, "That's my elegant girl. She was always ready to tell others about me, Father. I know her– she is mine. Well done, my good, faithful servant. Welcome home!"

I pray that the next time you are faced with a frustrating, unfair, or inconveniencing situation; you will choose to look beyond what it appears to be by human standards and see the heavenly opportunity presented to you. Perhaps your influence in another person's life will be the game-changer, allowing Christ to rescue them from a life of hopelessness and despair.

While you are standing in a long shopping line or sitting in heavy traffic, practice quietly praying for those around you while you wait. Be willing to trust God with your schedule. He wants your life to be a good one. He wants your days to be fruitful for His glory.

Perhaps you lack confidence to share Christ. Relax, you must simply make yourself available at all times and believe that He is able to equip you for the task at hand. You are becoming a woman of interior elegance: a work in progress. Remember you are not becoming in your own power. No need to shrink back into insecurities because the power of heaven is living inside of you, my beautiful, elegant sister. He is enough! Trust Him. Look for opportunities to share the wonderful gift of eternal life through Christ. I can assure you, whatever attempt you make for his glory will be *"good enough!"*

THE ELEGANT WOMAN OF GOD CONFESSES JESUS AS LORD.

Always be prepared to give an answer to everyone who asks you to give the reason for the hope that you have. But do it with gentleness and respect.
1 Peter 3:15 (NIV)

If you confess with your mouth, "Jesus is Lord," and believe in your heart that God raised Him from the dead, you will be saved. For it is with your heart that you believe and are justified, and it is with your mouth that you confess and are saved. Romans 10:9-10 (NIV)

ELEGANT REFLECTIONS

Reread Romans 10:9-10 (NIV): *If you confess with your mouth, "Jesus is Lord," and believe in your heart that God raised him from the dead, you will be saved. For it is with your heart that you believe and are justified, and it is with your mouth that you confess and are saved.*

It is with our heart that we believe and are justified. What does this mean to you?

_____
_____
_____
_____
_____

Have you confessed with your mouth that Jesus is Lord? If not, ask Him to come into your heart right now. You do not have to use elegant words. Be real. Be you. Write your invitation to Jesus on the lines below. Perhaps you have been a believer for many years but you want to rededicate your heart to Him.

_____
_____
_____
_____
_____

Do you have road rage? Does sitting in heavy traffic cause you to act in inelegant ways? Do you get frustrated if you are forced to wait in line at the grocery? Write how you respond to these scenarios here:

_____
_____
_____
_____
_____

Note: You are becoming a woman of interior elegance. Your thought life is slowly transforming. Your thoughts influence the way you react to people and situations.

How might you retrain your thinking when faced with frustrating situations beyond your control?

_____
_____
_____
_____
_____

Having a determined heart to change is the first step in real transformation. While reading the chapter entitled: *Good Enough,* how were you inspired, or convicted?

_____
_____
_____
_____
_____

Read: 1 Peter 3:15 (NIV). Are you prepared to give an answer for the hope you have?

_____
_____
_____
_____
_____

Note: You might feel inadequate after reading this chapter because your personality will not allow you to be quite as bold in sharing the gospel. I want you to remember: in the body of Christ there is no competition or comparison. The body of Christ is to complete each other. Perhaps the Lord is calling you to become a prayer-warrior for those around you when faced with frustrating inconveniences like the ones we have discussed here. Write your thoughts in the lines below:

_____

_____

_____

_____

Prayer: "Father, give me wisdom to know when you have positioned me in a particular setting to be used for your glory. Give me spiritual eyes to see beyond the external frustrations of life. Teach me to see life through spiritual eyes. I want to share my faith with others. Equip me to do so. I know you are good and you will receive my best efforts as good enough. Thank you, Father." Amen.

CHAPTER THIRTY-SEVEN

BRING BACK THOSE DYING DREAMS

If you enjoy dramatic, good reads, go to the word of God. In almost every chapter of the Bible, you will find extreme drama.

In the book of John, Chapter 11, Mary and Martha's brother Lazarus had died. The two sisters sent for Jesus while Lazarus was sick but Jesus lingered for a few more days before coming to their aide.

Want to talk about a real life nightmare?

Mary and Martha were shocked by Jesus' lack of response. They were after all, dear friends, having broken bread together while enjoying sweet fellowship in their home. Mary, Martha, and Lazarus believed in Christ's power and trusted Him greatly. But now, one nightmarish question lingered in the hearts of these two sisters. *Why had Jesus failed to come?*

Lazarus had been in the tomb for four days. Panic and disappointment overcame them. They cried out in grief-filled despair to Jesus when He finally arrived on the scene: *"If only you had been here Jesus, our brother would not have died."* From their perspective, He had arrived too late. The body would have begun the decaying process. But Jesus knew a greater glory would be revealed to those who questioned His authority as the Savior of the world. He came with a clear purpose in mind–to raise Lazarus from the grave. Compassion flowed freely and He wept, having felt their pain.

Perhaps you can identify with Mary and Martha. The wait has been long for you. You perceive God has forgotten your need, and you feel it's too late. You cry out in the midst of what feels like nightmarish, emotional pain. You have prayed all the prayers you could think to pray and did everything you could think to do. You are left wondering where Jesus is. Why has He not come to your aide? Perhaps you feel your dreams have died, been wrapped in grave cloth, and the stone has been rolled over the entrance of your heart's door.

Be encouraged today, sweet friend, as I remind you Christ has not overlooked your need. He is at work right now, fulfilling His perfect, purposed plan. He weeps with you as He sees your pain.

Jesus called out to his friend, saying, *"Lazarus, come forth!"* The One who came to conquer death and the grave had called Lazarus by name. Death could not hold him back.

Did you think it is too late? Even if your dreams have been rotting for four days, or four years, and you can smell the stench—it is not too late for Jesus, the Son of God to bring them back to life. You have been held captive long enough. Today is a brand new day. Believe and see the glory of God being revealed in your life as you rise to a new occasion. He is calling you out of the tomb. He has the power to resurrect our dead dreams, but only in His timing

He is near you now. Close your eyes and whisper the name of Jesus. Can you envision Him weeping as He sees *your pain?* Do you hear Him calling *your* name?

"_____*Come Forth!*"

The nightmare ends when we trust Him to complete every good thing He has purposed!

THE ELEGANT WOMAN OF BELIEVES GOD CAN COMMAND HER DREAMS TO *COME FORTH*.

When he had said these things, He cried out with a loud voice, "Lazarus, come forth." John 11:43 (NAS)

Featured article written by La-Tan Roland Murphy
Published in WHOA women Magazine/Summer 2013 Edition
www.WHOAwomen.com
(This is a revised version)

ELEGANT REFLECTIONS

Read John 11. Poor Mary and Martha, can you identify with them in any way?

_____

_____

_____

_____

Do you feel your dreams have died?

_____

_____

_____

_____

Christ's power is available to you. Ask him to command the dead places of your life to come forth. Write down what you would like Christ to resurrect in your life.

_____

_____

_____

_____

Christ wept when He saw his friends hurting. He weeps for you as well. How does this make you feel?

_____

_____

_____

_____

What need do you feel Jesus has over-looked? Be completely honest. Write in the space below:

_____

_____

_____

_____

Perhaps you have prayed for a long time for a specific thing. Do you feel like Mary and Martha—wondering why Jesus has delayed your answer to prayer? Perhaps you feel like Jesus failed to show up in your time of need. Write your thoughts below:

_____

_____

_____

_____

Do you have extreme drama happening in your life right now and you need Jesus to show up for you?

_____

_____

_____

_____

Prayer: "Father, I pray you will resurrect any dead place you see in my life that needs new life. I want to be alive in You, Jesus. Please call any dead dream that is in line with your perfect will for my life out of the grave." Amen.

CHAPTER THIRTY-EIGHT

A BEAUTIFUL PLAN GONE WRONG

Heavy fog impaired our vision, causing us to miss the main road leading to the camp site. We were forced onto a narrow path laced with sharp switchbacks that gave little warning. Still, we felt grateful for precious time away. I smiled as I glanced back, the children sleeping soundly. They were oblivious to the wind gusts rocking our car side to side as we went higher up the mountain.

I had carefully planned the perfect vacation. Excitement grew with each passing day leading up to this one. Camping in the beautiful North Carolina Mountains with my family thrilled my heart. I envisioned a cozy open fire, majestic mountain views, and fresh air kissing my contented face as I sat sipping hot java with loved ones.

We finally arrived after midnight. The headlights caught glimpses of flattened tents. Harsh winds whipped through the trees and continued to shake our car as we sat wondering where everyone was. After realizing they were all asleep *inside* the flattened tents, we determined it pointless to attempt setting our tent up. So, we settled into a miserable night of shivering as the bitter cold wind forced its way through every crack in the car.

Second night, tent up! I smiled wearily, drifting off in hopeful slumber. *Surely the rest of the trip would be less chaotic.* Much to my dismay, minutes into my optimistic slumber, the sound of gagging awakened me. My daughter was terribly sick–having eaten one too many Oreos and grilled hotdogs. Offensive odors snuggled into our borrowed tent, though I tried feverishly to clean it up. With all water pipes frozen, there was little I could do. Needless to say, my beautifully planned camping trip had turned into miserable mayhem.

Can you identify? Has there been a time in your life when your beautiful plan turned into chaotic misery? Are you frustrated and tired of watching the plans of others succeed like perfect Hallmark moments? While their journey seems smooth, yours has one harsh switchback after another with cold, bitter winds threatening to flatten your dreams?

You are not alone, friend. Put your faith in God today. He will be with you, even when your beautiful plans fail. He has far better plans than any you could conjure up! His peace will strengthen you for the journey. He is the light of the world, illuminating each dark, bitter night you will ever face.

I challenge you to read the word of God and identify with others whose plans were dashed in defeat and despair. Notice how, as they put their faith in Jesus, the Son of God, their joy was made complete as perfect peace overtook chaos. Higher places await you, dear friend. He will keep your heart encouraged regardless of imperfect scenarios. Today, He offers you...a beautiful plan that can't go wrong. Trust Him!

THE ELEGANT WOMAN OF GOD LIVES ACCORDING TO GOD'S PLAN.

A Beautiful Plan Gone Wrong

For I know the plans I have for you," declares the LORD, "plans to prosper you and not to harm you. Jeremiah 29:11 (NIV)

Featured article written by La-Tan Roland Murphy
Published in WHOA women Magazine/Spring 2013
www.WHOAwomen.com

ELEGANT REFLECTIONS

Have you ever planned a vacation? You imagined how perfect it would be, but when you arrived, everything went wrong? Write about it in the space below:

_____

_____

_____

_____

Perhaps you feel disappointed in the way your entire life has gone. If so, share in the space below:

_____

_____

_____

_____

Do you have a plan in your heart that you would like the Lord to bless and prosper? Write your desire in the space below.

_____

_____

_____

_____

Note: If we are to become women of interior elegance, we must make a commitment to the Lord to love and serve Him, no matter how our plans fall apart. Are you willing to serve the Lord no matter what? Write your commitment in the space below:

_____

_____

_____

_____

Have you ever been bitter because it seemed every else's life was a hallmark moment?

_____

_____

_____

_____

Have you ever been delayed? You were annoyed because you had planned to arrive at your destination on time. Did you realize later God had kept you from an accident or protected you in some way, by not allowing your plan to go perfectly?

_____

_____

_____

_____

Prayer: "Father, I confess your plans are far better than mine. Help me to trust You, even when I can't understand." Amen.

CHAPTER THIRTY-NINE

YOU DID GOOD BABY

He was tall and handsome. I was smitten, desperately wanting to impress him. So when he came to my home in Georgia to meet my family for the first time, I was a nervous wreck. My parents knew this was much more than a crush. They had never seen me this concerned about how clean the house was. I cleaned like a crazy person—even made sure the yard was as close to perfect as possible. But there was one problem: Daddy's old car.

It was an old Ford Country Squire station wagon, adorned with faded, veneered wood-grain panels. I stood with my arms crossed, looking it over from top to bottom, and then quickly devised a solution. *"Dad will be so surprised,"* I thought to myself, while reaching for the half-empty can of shellac in my Daddy's storage area. Although it was one of the hottest days of summer, my teenaged determination could not be deterred. Everything had to be perfect.

"Look Daddy! Doesn't your car look brand new? Look how shiny it is!"

"Oh baby, it's shiny alright! But honey, when the heat of summer beams down…those wood panels–they will crack like a jig-saw-puzzle."

My face must have revealed the disappointment and feelings of failure that were going on inside me. It was as though my Daddy saw inside every pocket of my heart. He saw my intentions clearly. His blue eyes met mine. Compassion flowed from his heart to mine. He gently put his arm around my shoulder.

"You did good, baby."

My Dad extended grace instead of the punishment I deserved.

Do you feel like a failure today? Perhaps you tried with all of your might to do something good, but feel your efforts weren't good enough. Do you feel like God is angry with you and holding a grudge? Trust me, compassion flows freely from His heart to yours.

He loves you, sweet friend. His love is the ever-lasting kind of love. It is not based on whether or not you do everything perfectly. You need not paint a coat of shellac on any faded, worn-out place in your life. He knows every road you have traveled and the effort it took to get this far. He sees you and He sees the intent of your heart. Let your determination be fixed on pleasing Christ, only. Someday when you stand before Him, you will hear Him say:

"You did good, baby."

THE ELEGANT WOMAN OF GOD IS GRATEFUL FOR THE LORD'S COMPASSION IN LIGHT OF HER HUMAN FRAILTY.

Then the Lord was gracious to them and had compassion and showed concern for them because of his covenant with Abraham, Isaac and Jacob.
2 Kings 13:23 (NIV)

ELEGANT REFLECTIONS

What were your thoughts about the story entitled: *You Did Good, Baby?*
Write your thoughts in the space below:

_____

_____

_____

_____

Note: My Daddy offered grace even though I didn't really deserve it. I
had messed up his car terribly. Most people would have expressed anger.
But, Daddy chose grace.

How does Christ offer grace that is undeserved?

_____

_____

_____

_____

Note: The shellac did not change the interior of my Daddy's car. It was
only a shiny veneer, covering the real issues beneath. How might we do
the same thing, spiritually speaking? Write your answer in the space
below:

_____

_____

_____

_____

Note: My Dad had every reason to be angry with me. He could have crushed my spirit that day, had he responded the way most people would have. If he had been verbally abusive or responded in extreme anger, our relationship could have been altered. Because he chose to offer grace and had the wisdom to know my emotional well-being was more important than his car, he left a deep mark on my life for Christ. I tried very hard while raising my own children to think before reacting. What have you learned from this?

_____

_____

_____

_____

Prayer: "Father, thank you for offering grace when I deserved your punishment. Thank you for loving me and for seeing my heart. Thank you for receiving my well-intended offerings, even when I fall short." Amen.

CHAPTER FORTY

A WINDOW WITH A VIEW

The morning sunlight seemed to dance off of everything it touched like a synchronized, shimmering light show—glowing, flittering—light touching every plant and tree; still, I could not embrace its glory and beauty because, I was stuck. Yes, stuck in the past with regret welling up from deep within me. "If only"... "I should have"... "I wish I would have"... "Why didn't I?"

Then, much like an old movie reel, memories began to roll out before me. The crackling, black and white views of my past taunting me as one remorseful clip replaced the next. Mistakes and missed opportunities competing for my attention—each flashing before me as I stared out the window, wasting the gorgeous view of yet another brand-new day. All because I was allowing myself to be held hostage by the little mental and emotional prison I had created for myself. All the while, God was waiting and longing to give me a window with a view. He wanted me to see beyond the little prison walls I had created for myself, to His future purpose.

We simply cannot grab hold of the future Christ has for us until we stop looking back. I can't begin to tell you how much of my life I have wasted focusing on past mistakes. Although I knew I had been forgiven and was a new creation in Christ, I would often end up looking back regretfully.

No matter what your past looks like, my friend, I have good news for you today! Each morning we are given the fresh beauty of a brand new day. If we wake up, that means we are still breathing. If we are breathing, this is a good indication that God has a big plan with us in mind. He is a gentleman and never forces himself on us. God offers choices because He is the essence of *freedom*. When we make the conscious, wise choice to follow Him and live according to His holy word, He then equips us with wisdom to face each day. The things in our past—regrets and failures, only serve to remind us of the places Christ has rescued us from and delivered us out of. Our story becomes His glory, as we choose to tell others our testimony. Powerful things begin happening at that point.

As we grow into women of interior elegance, we must focus our attention on the ONE who knew no sin. He took on our sin, so that we could be free from the little daily prisons we create for ourselves. Each time we think to ourselves: *"We aren't enough,"* He says: *"I'll be enough for you, my daughter!"*

The Israelite people had their struggles also. We can identify with them as we read of their journey through the desert. Even though a wicked Pharaoh had held them in captivity for 400 years, they too had become comfortable in familiar prisons and bondages. Although God was offering them something far greater than they had ever envisioned, like us, they too struggled in their flesh and focused on themselves. They were distracted by reflections of the past: the figs, the pomegranates, and other choice foods they had while imprisoned there in Egypt. They had forgotten the shackles, the bondage, and the harsh cruelty they suffered. God had offered them a new life and set them on a new path towards a promise land, offering them a window with a view. Yet all they could do was look back: distracted by their own reflection in the window as they whined, complained, and wore themselves out. The heat of the desert and the hunger in their bellies kept them from looking out and beyond to the hope-filled life, offering true freedom in the beauty of Canaan. God had brought them through the desert, provided manna from heaven, and even put a cloud of protection over them by day and by night. But, like us, they became distracted, lost their faith, and they lost their strength for the journey because of their relentless grumbling. However, when the faithful ones chose to look beyond their own reflection in the window and live by faith, reflecting on the goodness of God and how He had brought them through, they slowly began to see the view God was trying to offer them all along. Then finding renewed strength of purpose, hope, and power, they rejoiced in the God of freedom as they entered the Promise land.

Our Challenge:

- To never allow ourselves to be defeated by our past. *"Behold I make all things new!"* Rev. 21:5 (NIV)
- To look back only for the purpose of rejoicing in the fact that we made it through every desert place!
- To live a life that welcomes His PROTECTIVE hand.
- To welcome God's transforming power, as we become women of deep conviction.
- To practice hearing God's voice in our lives and keep our spirits tender.
- To strive to be women willing to OBEY the commands of God, walking upright with uncompromising faith.
- To allow Christ's power to ultimately reset the course of our life choices, both simple and complex, to be choices HE would approve of and bless.
- To be on guard through prayer against the enemy as he tries to fill us with despair, weaken our defenses, or cause us to become distracted with reflections of our past that seek to rob our faith, hope, joy, and purpose.
- To Praise Him for His watchful care over us in the past, knowing we never would have made it this far without Him.

I pray as you reflect on the goodness of God and how He brought you through, you will find strength for each and every day. Allow Him to refocus your attention beyond your circumstances to the hope that is yours in Christ. I promise the view will be breath-taking.

Featured article by La-Tan Roland Murphy
Published in WHOA women Magazine/Winter 2013 Edition
www.WHOAwomen.com
(This is a revised version)

ELEGANT REFLECTIONS

Do you struggle to forget your sinful past?

_____
_____
_____
_____
_____
_____

Note: God wants to give you a window with a view. He does not want you to be held captive by emotional prison walls.

What prison walls have you created for yourself? Confess on the lines below:

_____
_____
_____
_____
_____
_____

Write down how God has been speaking to you.

_____
_____
_____
_____
_____
_____

How has Christ changed your view of life?

_____
_____
_____
_____
_____
_____

Read Revelations 21:5. Christ makes all things new. What has Christ made new for you?

_____
_____
_____
_____
_____
_____

What does it mean to "be on-guard against the enemy's schemes?"

_____
_____
_____
_____
_____
_____

How does Christ literally reset the course of our life choices?

_____
_____
_____
_____
_____
_____

How can we identify with the Israelite's journey through the desert?

_____

_____

_____

_____

_____

_____

Prayer: "Father, I praise your name. You have helped reset the course of my life by offering the gift of your son, Jesus. Thank you for the power of heaven you freely gave. Thank you for giving me a window with a view. Thank you for freeing me from the walls of bondage I had built around myself." Amen.

Chapter Forty-One

ABUNDANT LIFE

When the economy crashed, people lost jobs, homes, and retirement savings. Many other financial comforts were stripped away from hardworking Americans. Things that were deemed evidence of abundant living before the economy crashed no longer exist.

My husband and I were among those who had the veil lifted, as we realized our vision had been blurred by the American dream. A sobering reality check does that you know–snatches you by the nape of your neck, drawing you back into reality. When all the veneers were stripped away, we were able to gage abundance by a very different set of standards.

Our family feels blessed as we reminisce about the peace that passed all understanding given us during our financial hard times. Many circumstances threatened to rob us of joy, hope, and future. God's provision in tough times redefined our idea of abundance in more ways than one. We see clearly now that abundant life begins with:

- **Acknowledgement of our human frailty in light of God's magnificent power**

- **Faith to trust in His provision**
- **Surrendering control**
- **Realizing God sees our needs and promises to provide for those who put their faith in Him. (How could the creator of all things be anything short of abundant?)**

The peace that comes with total surrender is amazing. Friend, I want to encourage you to trust Christ's power and provision. When you've done all you know to do, after having worked your fingers to the bone, your heavenly Father will fill in the gaps. He will make frayed ends meet that would otherwise, never be met.

Perhaps you feel abundance skipped past your house to the neighbors. Perhaps you've been wasting your days peeking through the neighbor's fence, wondering how they got it all. Perhaps you are feeling sorry for yourself as you read this.

The abundant life goes way beyond what the checkbook says. As we redefine abundance by God's standards, we are able to intentionally notice blessings we once overlooked in times of plenty. Do you have your health, a loving family, a roof over your head, and/or good friends who stand with you when life gets hard? Sure sounds like abundance to me.

It has been said: *You make a living by what you get, but you make a life by what you give.* True abundance hinges on one thing: *how* you live your life. If you aren't blessed with financial abundance, you can be blessed with the abundant joy of giving out of what you have been given.

Friends, take time to listen to the birds sing. You won't hear them singing the blues or wringing their feathers out with worry for provision. Their songs do not include fearful melodies about losing their nest, or wanting a bigger and better nest. They are content—their daily needs provided for. Trust God to supply your every need; He measures abundance by different standards than we do. Believe and stand firmly on the power of God's word. Welcome to the true abundant life!

THE ELEGANT WOMAN OF GOD FINDS ABUNDANCE IN CHRIST ALONE.

So don't be afraid; you are more valuable to God than a whole flock of sparrows.
Matthew 10:31 (NIV)

Featured article written by La-Tan Roland Murphy
Originally entitled: Hard Times, Happier Times
Published in WHOA women Magazine/Fall 2013 Edition
www.WHOAwomen.com
(This is a revised version with title change)

ELEGANT REFLECTIONS

Do you feel like abundance skipped past your home?

_____
_____
_____
_____
_____
_____

What is abundance by the world's standard?

_____
_____
_____
_____
_____
_____

What is abundance by God's standard?

_____
_____
_____
_____
_____
_____

Reread Matthew 10:31 (NIV): *So don't be afraid; you are more valuable to God than a whole flock of sparrows.*

Do you worry about provision?

_____
_____
_____
_____
_____
_____

Look back across the years, how did God prove Himself as your provider?

_____

_____

_____

_____

_____

_____

You are precious to your heavenly Father. He promises to take care of those who put their hope and trust in Him. Are you doing so?

_____

_____

_____

_____

_____

_____

Do you struggle to trust God for your daily provision?

_____

_____

_____

_____

_____

_____

Note: I love watching birds. They sing and flitter, but they do not worry about food or shelter.

Let's practice singing when we are worried or stressed. Have you ever done this? How did singing change your stress level?

_____

_____

_____

_____

_____

_____

Prayer: "Father, thank you for providing for all of my needs according to your great riches in Christ. Teach me to rest in your goodness. I know you will supply all of my needs. Thank you for teaching me how to live in your abundant love and grace. Help me to stop worrying about tomorrow." Amen.

CHAPTER FORTY-TWO

HECTOR

I am terrified of large dogs. Actually, I have been fearful since I was about 8 years old—the day our neighbor's enormous German shepherd—knocked me off my bike. I could feel the massive animal's hot breath against my skin as I lay on the dirt road, trembling. What large teeth it had!

That single moment contributes to my overwhelming and often paralyzing fear, experienced every time I go to a dog-owner's home. This fear is related to the mere presence of a dog, but if the dog comes out barking, well…that just kicks my fear-factor to a whole other level altogether! A pleasant walk in my neighborhood can quickly turn into a stressful occasion with the sound of one single bark, especially if the dog is off its owner's leash.

Hector is a large pit bull. His broad shoulders intimidate and dominate. Hector belongs to my son's friend, Troy. Troy went out of town for Christmas one year and asked my son, Kyle, to keep Hector for him. When we called to invite Kyle and his wife, Carolyn, to come home for Christmas, they said yes. But someone else had to come with them. You guessed right! Hector would be coming to my house for Christmas! Merry Christmas to ME!

I did after all, have very good reason to be fearful of Hector. My husband witnessed first-hand the strength of Hectors jaws the day my son tossed a tennis ball in his direction. Giant muscles became air born and sharp teeth snatched the ball in mid-air, effortlessly snapping the whole of it into two pieces as though it were play dough. In fact, Hector has been known to snap a large tree limb in half. The wag of his tail can knock a child completely down–not to mention make this grown woman's heart pound at a rapid rate when the gut-wrenching anxiety of his presence near me takes hold.

What is a good mother to do when given the choice between her children not coming home for Christmas or coming with Hector, the pit bull with the massive shoulders and head? So...I put on my big-girl panties and made a conscious decision to deal with my nerves, head-on.

I told my husband that God surely has a sense of humor. I had prayed a prayer just a week or so before Hector's arrival—asking the Lord to re-move any fear that might exist in my life, so that I might serve Him with boldness. Little did I know that Hector was part of God's plan—bring-ing me face-to-face with a ghost from my past that had long held me captive emotionally and perhaps spiritually, as well. This fear was more than just fear of dogs. It was fear of reaching into the future, believing I could accomplish amazing things. It represented fear of failure, fear of being alone, fear of acceptance, as well as many other faces of fear that flash before me as I write this.

Can you identify with me? Have you ever been afraid to venture out, try some new adventure in life and step out in faith, believing in the gifts and abilities the Lord has given you? Maybe as you read this you are flat on your back, with fear breathing into your face-its teeth growing bigger and bigger as you become paralyzed by its presence. Just because Hector is at your house for Christmas doesn't mean he is staying. Soon your unwanted houseguest will have to leave. Fear cannot dominate you any more than you allow it to. Ask the Lord to take every thought captive by the power of His son, Jesus. He is faithful to do just that! Even Hector's ferocious bark, broad shoulders and giant jaws are nothing in light of the power of your heavenly Father. He is perfect love, manifested in the form of a savior who came into the world to remove fear and anything else that stands in the way of God's best for our lives.

THE ELEGANT WOMAN OF GOD ALLOWS CHRIST'S POWER TO CONQUER HER FEARS.

Be strong and courageous. Do not be afraid or terrified of them, for the Lord your God goes with you. He will never leave you nor forsake you.
Deuteronomy 31:6 (NIV)

ELEGANT REFLECTIONS

Do you have a Hector in your life?

_____

_____

_____

_____

What are you most fearful of?

_____

_____

_____

_____

How has fear paralyzed you?

_____

_____

_____

_____

Christ's power helps us conquer fear. Let's agree to claim His power to-day. Write your claim in the space below:

_____

_____

_____

_____

Write down one thing you wish you could do if fear were not a factor in your life?

_____

_____

_____

_____

Ask the Lord to empower you and help you to conquer all fear in your life.

_____

_____

_____

_____

Reread Deuteronomy 31:6: *Be strong and courageous. Do not be afraid or terrified of them. For the Lord your God is with you. He will not leave you nor forsake you.*

What comfort do you find in this word?

_____

_____

_____

_____

Prayer: "Father, release me from fear. Give me a courageous heart. Help me to not be terrified of anyone, or anything. I know you are standing watch." Amen.

CHAPTER FORTY-THREE

I WATCHED YOU

Holiday traditions are memorable. But the most cherished traditions are the simple, daily things we do with our family and friends that often seem insignificant.

As the last of my three children leave home, a bittersweet glimpse of my future empty nest is before me. *'Mother Memory'* reaches deep within the pockets of my heart, pulling out one sentimental memory after another and bringing on an 'ugly cry!' I have been down this road before... twice in fact, as my first two children are married.

Family traditions fill me with deep emotion as the sweetest life moments come crashing onto the shore of my sentimental heart from my ocean of treasured memories: Valentine card making, ginger bread houses, and Easter baskets set outside of each bedroom door–filled with candy to please each individual taste. Surprise 'pajama runs' through drive-thru windows for late night ice cream treats. Rainy day cookies, much to blame for the extra weight I still carry...especially since it rained for two weeks straight with my children doing a rain dance under every potential rain cloud in the sky.

Did I waste my time on silly things that mattered only to *me*? Did anyone notice *anything*?

Joy filled my heart the day I received a text with a picture of home-made cookies and a simple message from my only daughter that read: ***Rainy Day Cookies…I WATCHED YOU…***

While I was beating myself up, wishing I could buy or do more, she was busy collecting memories–stowing away traditions that would come back to me someday as a sweet surprise…entitled:

Warwickshire Way
By: DaNae Murphy

"Home is where the heart is." We've all heard it said before—yet most of us choose to leave it. Unfortunately, it takes distance sometimes to realize just how true that statement is. Not necessarily for everyone but for me.

When I think about home the first thing that pops into my head isn't the town but more the people that live there. The people I grew up with. The people that made an impact on my life shaping me into who I am, took a chance on me, believed in me, made me think I could go anywhere, do anything, dream as big as I wanted. I'll even go as far as saying, the people who hurt me growing up over the years because that's what it takes for us to learn how to become strong in who we are. All of their names are forever tattooed on my heart and I thank them for loving me. Home looks like something different to everyone. It could be something good or something you have been trying to run away from. Some may not even remember much about home or never had one. I have so much to thank God for especially the home he blessed me with and the memories I have with my family that loves me. If mind reading was possible and you could get inside my head flipping through my lifetime you might find something like this…

- **Warm chocolate chip cookies on a rainy day**
- **The smell of mulch and freshly cut grass**
- **Scabs from brakeless roller blades**
- **A tree that seemed impossible to climb**
- **The smell of mint in my grandmother's closet**

- A secret drawer of candy stocked with white mints and chocolate
- Saturday morning cartoons and cream horns
- A secret 3-story tree house and a sandbox full of dead frogs—victims—playing the role of prince in my sand castles
- A white house with black shutters and a porch that is full of laughter, tears, breakups, sun bathing, wood bees killed with tennis rackets, and goodnight kisses
- A drive-way stained from an oil-leaking white jeep, sidewalk chalk, a trashcan at the end that I backed into way too many times—letting it fly into the neighbor's yard.
- (Sorry about that ;-))
- Late night couch conversations
- Shoes piled at the door
- Card games by the fire
- Family prayer before bed
- A dog named Mayci May who seems more like a sister—knowing all of my secrets
- Wooden stairs you can NEVER sneak down
- A wooded lot viewed from a big kitchen window pretty by day, scary by night.
- Pictures drawn on the wall behind my clothes in the closet and never enough shoes!
- Dance Revolution in the bonus room, movies with friends piled on the couch.
- The smell of cow pies, monkey bread, taste of homemade Oreo ice cream.

I haven't been all over the world, or tasted the finer things of life. I still don't have it all together but I'm learning that's okay. I am still young and have a lot to learn (and mom I'm still striving to be the brightest crayon in the box.) I'm building brand new memories as a married woman and hope to provide warm memories like these for my kids someday. Mom and Dad…. thank you, for raising me in a warm, Godly, welcoming environment and for making all these memories and many more, stepping-stones to the woman I've become. Home IS where the heart is and HOME is whatever you make it to be. I can't say where my feet will end up landing over the next 60 years but I know this…A piece of my heart will always be on Warwickshire Way.

THE ELEGANT WOMAN MAKES EVERY MINUTE COUNT, FOR THE GLORY OF GOD.

Be very careful then, how you live—not as unwise but as wise, making the most of every opportunity. Ephesians 5:15, 16 (NIV)

Featured article written by La-Tan Roland Murphy
Published in WHOA women Magazine/Fall 2012 Edition
www.WHOAwomen.com
(This is a revised version)

ELEGANT REFLECTIONS

Note: Make the most of each day, my friend. Our children are storing away rainy day memories inside cookie jars, filled with sweet traditions. You are a woman of influence. The things you do both great and small, make a difference! Remember: someone is *watching you!*

Reread Ephesians 5:15, 16 (NIV): *Be very careful then, how you live—not as unwise but as wise, making the most of every opportunity.*

How do you make the most of every opportunity in your life?

_____

_____

_____

_____

Note: Your influence in the lives of others is important. We have been given the choice of influencing those around us in positive ways or negative ways.

Do you influence people in positive ways or negative ways?

_____

_____

_____

_____

Who has influenced your life in the most positive way?

_____

_____

_____

_____

Write down your favorite childhood memories?

_____

_____

_____

_____

What is your favorite family tradition?

_____

_____

_____

_____

Why is it important to be wise?

_____

_____

_____

_____

Prayer: "Father, thank you for family traditions and for sweet memories that last a lifetime. Help me to live a life that is pleasing to you and one that will leave a positive, lasting mark." Amen.

CHAPTER FORTY-FOUR

MY GRANDMOTHER'S CHAIR

🐚

My grandmother's chair sat in the corner, to the right side of the fireplace. It was her special place to visit with friends and family.

From my perspective, the chair seemed magical. When my Grandmother—or 'Granny Mae,' as I lovingly referred to her, sat down in her special chair, it meant focused time spent with me was soon to be!

My grandmother was a pint-sized, little lady with piercing blue eyes as gentle as her spirit. She was a woman of few words, yet her heart and actions screamed out to me: *I LOVE YOU unconditionally*, grabbing me by my invisible heart strings and making me beg to stay at her house each weekend.

We often sat side-by-side, she in her special chair and me in the wooden rocker I had claimed as *mine*; no television blaring loudly to fill the silent void, no radio noise wafting upward into the quiet recesses of the twelve-foot ceilings—just my sweet little 'Granny Mae' and me, enjoying the quiet.

Her life was balanced. She knew when to work and when to stop working. Scurrying around late at night in order to put one more load of laundry in, or talking on the phone incessantly was not part of her plan to renew herself. Instead, each night after dinner, she sat in her favorite chair in order to relax, and pamper herself. I loved watching her comb her never-been-cut hair, which hung down below her lower back in length. I was mesmerized, watching as she braided and then wrapped each strand around her head, securing it firmly with bobby pins.

After her beauty routine, she would often reach for her Bible. Etched in my mind, to this day, is the black leather cover, worn from years of use, its pages curled and faded. "Read something to me," she would say, with a warm smile and a twinkle in her eye. From my perspective, she needed me.

I sat straight and tall in my chair–proudly reading passage after passage. When I completed what I thought was my last sentence, she would say, "Read on…" and so I would read on, until I was sure she was content. I remember thinking that this was my gift to her—little did I know it was her gift to me! In her wisdom, she knew God's word would never go void, once entering into my heart. The twinkle in her eyes must have been the reflection of sheer joy in knowing the power she was handing over to me, each time she placed her Bible in my small hands. For my heart was becoming renewed and refreshed by the word of God. As each word spilled from my mouth into her listening ears—we were both changed and made new. Her focused effort to live a balanced life proved to be a blessing to us both! She worked hard, but she also knew when to stop and reflect.

I am reminded of a story found in God's word expressing the importance of sitting in God's presence. In Luke 10:38-42, Jesus had arrived at the home of Mary's sister, Martha. Martha did not have a clear understanding of the importance of taking time out of her busy schedule in order to be renewed. Busyness ruled her days. Like many of us, she had lost her sense of balance. Her work, though a good thing, had become a source of distraction. But Mary, Martha's sister, slipped away from the kitchen, away from the busyness, in order to sit at the feet of the one whose words held the power to renew her entire being. Martha complained, saying Mary was being lazy. It was this martyrdom, complaining spirit that provoked Jesus to rebuke Martha in verse 41: *"Martha, Martha, you are worried and upset about many things but only one thing is needed. Mary has chosen what is better and it will not be taken away from her."*

God's Holy word does not go void. You might feel like everything has been taken from you and nothing is going right. Perhaps your marriage has fallen apart. Your children's lives did not turn out the way you thought they would. Are you busy trying to simply survive, wondering, *"How can I sit down? If I don't do these things, no one else will!"*

I want to challenge you to find a special chair; sit quietly and reflectively in the presence of the Savior. If you do this, you will have chosen the better thing. Time spent with God is time well-spent. It will renew you, and give you strength and wisdom—helping you make wise decisions.

Perhaps you have never asked Christ to come into your heart, ask Him today! Then take the Bible in your hands and, as my grandmother said to me, *"Read on..."*

These days, you can find my grandmother's chair sitting in my living room to the right side of our fireplace. It represents much more than just a beautiful antique with intricate carvings. It serves to remind me:

- **To set aside time each day to sit down, perhaps in a special chair, in order to reflect and give thanks to God.**
- **To slow down and focus on balancing work with times of renewal.**
- **To prioritize reading God's word.**
- **To acknowledge the power of God's word.**
- **To remember the importance of placing God's word in the hands of others who are hopeless and in need of renewing power.**

- **To be still and know that He is God!**

I am so thankful for the fact that my grandmother chose the 'better thing.' I am a life that was changed; because she took time out of her busy life in order to place the worn, black book with its curled up pages into my small, willing hands.

Perhaps you did not have someone in your life who would take time out of his or her busy schedule in order to offer you the sweet, renewing power of God's word. I want to encourage your heart today, my friend. You can *be* that person! Find a special chair, take time out of your busy life, sit with the word of God in your hands, and be renewed by its life-giving power. Who knows, there might even be a child somewhere who would be willing to sit next to you and 'read on' so you can both be renewed in His presence!

THE ELEGANT WOMAN OF GOD TAKES TIME OUT OF HER DAY TO SIT AT THE FEET OF JESUS.

Be still and know that I am God. Psalm 46:10 (NIV)

Featured article written by La-Tan Roland Murphy and published in
WHOA women Magazine/Spring 2012 Edition
www.WHOAwomen.com
(This article is a revised edition)

ELEGANT REFLECTIONS

Read Luke 10:38-42.

Are you most like Mary or Martha?

_____
_____
_____
_____

Do you feel you have a good balance between work and play?

_____
_____
_____
_____

Note: My grandmother led a balanced life. What valuable lesson did you learn from reading this story?

_____
_____
_____
_____

Reread Psalm 46:10. Write in the space below how you might rearrange your life in order to be still and know that He is God?

_____
_____
_____
_____

Do you read God's word on a regular basis? If so, write in the space given below how it helps you find balance. If you do not, then write in the space below your new commitment to dedicate yourself to the reading of God's word each day:

_____

_____

_____

_____

How might you mentor a younger person, in order to pass the torch of faith on to the next generation?

_____

_____

_____

_____

Prayer: "Father, teach me how to live a balanced life. I want to take time to rest and reflect on your goodness. Forgive me for not including you in my busy schedule. I praise you for the power of your holy word. Help me to never take it for granted." Amen.

CHAPTER FORTY-FIVE

WHAT'S YOUR ANACONDA?

My image was at risk as I ran through the cold, dark night—purse on my right shoulder—a personal delivery for my neighbor in my left hand. I dreaded the wooded lot separating our houses, especially at night. Recently having found a copperhead snake in our driveway only escalated my fear. Suddenly, I heard a noise rustling in the leaves behind me. Fear wrapped her long legs around my waist and would not let go! Inhibition left me. Caring not who saw me or how ridiculous I might have looked, I ran like a maniac! Leaping, feet lifted in the air— the Tennessee Walking Horses had nothing on me—toes pointed, knees pumping higher with each fearful step, screams synchronized with each leg change–all done in perfect rhythm. Fear-filled imaginations carried me off to ridiculous places. My thoughts ran together: *"It must be enormous...only a huge snake could make a noise this loud...it is seriously chasing me. It goes faster and faster as I pick up speed...I am sure it is an anaconda!"*

By the time I reached my neighbors home, I was huffing and puffing—as only an out-of-shape, fifty-year-old woman can after sprinting through an ocean of dead leaves in the dark of night. Pride-fully, I thanked God it *was* night, cringing at the thought of the neighbors peeking out their windows. How humiliating!

As I reached the top of the porch steps, a strange sound startled me. "Clunk-clunk…" I swallowed hard, took a deep breath, and peered back over my shoulder. My eyes dropped slowly downward, following the hanging cord spilling from the backside of my purse—leading all the way down to the porch step. A small black box attached to its end had come to rest after slithering through the black of the night behind me. Disbelief left me speechless! *My oversized anaconda was not what it had appeared to be after all*! It was in fact, the cord of my cell phone charger!

What's your anaconda, friend?

- **Are you running scared from something that threatens to mar your image?**
- **Have you allowed a grim situation to keep you on the run, while the snake in the leaves has grown bigger and bigger in your mind?**
- **Are you exhausted from running scared because each time you look in the mirror, the enemy tells you that you will never be young or beautiful again?**
- **Do you compare yourself to something that does not exist—like airbrushed images and computerized perfection? 2 Corinthians 4:16 (NIV):** *We do not lose heart, though outwardly we are wasting away, yet inwardly we are being renewed day by day.*
- **Perhaps you have been running scared—powerless to restore your broken marriage. Your self-image has been defined by your husband's responses to you. Perhaps your imaginary anaconda says: "If you were sexier, your husband wouldn't have left you for the younger woman?"**

My friend, I want to encourage you today: Your anaconda is not too big for Christ! Christ has the power to fill you with confidence and, as you acknowledge Him, your self-worth will be defined by what He has to say about you. He says you are beautiful in His sight, and you are enough! Psalm 91:14 (NIV): *Because she loves me", says the Lord, "I will rescue her; I will protect her, for she acknowledges my name.*

- **Perhaps you are running scared because your child refuses to make wise choices. You have tried with all your might to help set his or her life back on the right course.**

I Timothy 1:12 (NIV): *I know whom I have believed, and am convinced that He is able to guard what I have entrusted to Him for that* **day.**

As women, we are often our own worst enemy. Never did I imagine when I put my phone cord in my purse that morning that by evening it would have transformed into a *man-eating anaconda*. A bad self-image keeps us running in fear—creating imaginary anacondas that do not really exist. We feel alone in the pitch-dark night as our enemy slithers behind us. In reality, we are never alone. The one who created us is with us every step we take. He loves us with so great a love that He would lay down his life.

I challenge you to look for your self-worth in the one who created you and called you worthy. He loved you enough to send his one and only son, Jesus, to bear all of your sin and shame. You do not have to wait until you have it all together to come to Him. Romans 5:8 (NIV): *God demonstrates his own love for us in this: while we were still sinners, Christ died for us.*

Once we accept Christ as the way, the truth, and the life, the same anacondas that once tried so hard to keep us running fearfully lose their power in His presence. No longer will our self-image be based on imaginations or fearful thinking, but on the truth of God's word.

So what's your anaconda? Run! Run faster my friend, toward the image of Christ today. Knees up! Toes Pointed! I can almost hear Him say: *My daughter, THIS ANACONDA IS NOT TOO BIG FOR ME!*

THE ELEGANT WOMAN OF GOD IS NOT AFRAID.

I know whom I have believed, and am convinced that He is able to guard what I have entrusted to Him for that day. 2 Timothy 1:12 (NIV)

Featured article written by La-Tan Roland Murphy and published in
WHOAwomen Magazine/Summer 2012 Edition
www.WHOAwomen.com
(This is a revised version)

ELEGANT REFLECTIONS

What are you running from today?

_____
_____
_____
_____

What's your anaconda?

_____
_____
_____
_____

Reread II Corinthians 4:16 (NIV): *We do not lose heart, though outwardly we are wasting away, yet inwardly we are being renewed day by day.*

Do the words of II Corinthians 4:16 encourage you? If so, write about it in the space below:

_____
_____
_____
_____

Reread II Timothy 1:12 (NIV): *I know whom I have believed, and am convinced that He is able to guard what I have entrusted to Him for that day.*

Write in the space below what this means to you:

_____
_____
_____
_____

Reread Psalm 91:14 (NIV): *"Because she loves me," says the Lord, "I will rescue her; I will protect her, for she acknowledges my name."*

Share about how the power of God has rescued and/or protected you.

_____

_____

_____

_____

REMEMBER: THIS ANACONDA IS NOT TOO BIG FOR GOD!

How can a bad self-image keep us on the run?

_____

_____

_____

_____

Prayer: "Father, thank you for rescuing me and protecting me. I will not run in fear. I will run to you — my help, my rock, my fortress — in times of trouble." Amen.

CHAPTER FORTY-SIX

SWEET TEA WITH LEMONS

Afriend of mine shared with me that her husband seemed to be withdrawn from her. The change seemed to happen almost overnight. Once a great listener, now he rarely responded to her. I asked her to look within herself first, in order to see how she might have changed. It is so easy to look at others and see the change that has taken place in them, but we rarely take inventory of ourselves. She thought for a moment and then her eyes lit up as she said, "Sweet tea with lemon. I haven't made him sweet tea with lemon in a long time." Her answer surprised me. It was such a simple thing. She continued, "When I make him sweet tea with lemon, he acts like I have given him the moon!"

"Ok...now we are on to something...do your homework, girl," I said looking back over my shoulder, as I walked away. "Make the sweet tea and don't forget the lemon!"

The next time I saw her, she was grinning from ear to ear. "He loved it. I need to remember this! He has been treating me like I am the most incredible woman in the world!" she said, with a silly grin.

Remember when you were dating? If you were like me, you intentionally sought out ways to please your boyfriend. Your love and admiration ran so deep, and you simply couldn't imagine living life without him. Perhaps you whispered a private vow to love him forever and nurture the gift of him, always. You were determined never to take him for granted, right?

But much like the perfect dress you bought at the mall—the one you thought you just couldn't live without–you date him, marry him, bring him home and suddenly things aren't so perfect. Instead of spending your precious time and energy thinking of ways to show your love to him, you spend your time finding fault. Once filled with love and all the gushy feelings that go with it, you are now filled with anger and disappointment. You are shocked to find your charming prince turned back into the wart-covered toad after the honeymoon! Things spiral from here. Each day, instead of ministering to your man, you create misery for him as you constantly badger him about all the things he is doing wrong.

I remember doing this to my own husband early in our marriage. My frustration would build as he proceeded to roll his eyes in disgust each time I pulled my 'use to' list out of my memory bag. It read something like this: *"You use to want to sit and talk with me; you use to hold my hand and randomly hug me for no reason; you use to think I was wonderful; you use to tell me I looked pretty..."* I never considered the possibility that he might have a list of 'use to' of his own. Satan had my mind on one thing—ME!

An angry spirit began to rise up in my heart. I lost sight of the promise I had made to myself, and to him, when we fell in love. I had told him I would cherish him forever and never take him for granted. Without realizing it, I had stopped looking for special ways to please him the way I did when we were dating. No longer did I spend my time searching for ways to speak love to him. I had become fixated on the things he was not doing, rather than focusing on what he was doing!

We all know full well how the story goes...*Boy meets girl. They fall in love. They scramble for ways to make each other happy and promise to never take each other for granted. They get married and soon, the newness wears off. They become unfocused, no longer looking for ways to please each other or find special ways to express their love to one another. Excitement turns into anger. Soon the voice of the enemy begins to whispers lies, causing division.*

You see, sweet friend, the enemy thrives on creating division. He will go to great lengths to steal your joy. He knows the importance of unity in the marriage relationship, and the holiness the marriage union has the power to represent when two hearts are fully surrendered and intentional about keeping themselves grounded in God's word. The enemy tells us to not lift another finger to serve our man. This voice becomes louder and louder each time we give into it. The cycle continues: he seems unattached and distracted while we feel alone and unloved, then resentment begins to mount. Resistance, anger, and a bitter spirit melt our once tender, loving hearts down into a hardened state.

It is often those little, random acts of kindness that hold the most power to reopen gateways leading to closed-off hearts. Simple effort is one of the most powerful ways to make people feel loved and appreciated: consider them, notice them, and remember them. It is when we feel over-looked, neglected, and forgotten that the door to our hearts begins to close, little-by-little. Small things left undone become big.

There will be sour experiences to work through in any relationship. But you wouldn't think of serving the lemon without the tea, would you?

To some, the story of my friend and the sweet tea might seem silly. You might wonder, *"How can sweet tea with lemon make such a difference?"* My answer to you is this: Do whatever works for you…do it with all your heart! If keeping the house clean and organized is important to your husband, then work hard to honor him in keeping it clean. If stopping everything in order to spend uninterrupted time with your man at the end of the day is important to him, it should be important to you, *Martha!* So sit down and listen to what is on his heart. Someone must sow the seeds before the flowers can bloom. Be willing to be the first to make the extra effort, even if you don't get instant results. Every time we reach out in love, we have crushed the head of the enemy, Satan, and cleared the path for God's power to spring forth in our lives and in our marriages.

God has the power to take both the sweet and sour encounters and make our marriages the perfect blend. When we fully surrender the good and the bad, then the sour occasions in life hold potential for a wonderful mix from which to grow and learn. It is all up to us. How determined are we going to be in keeping our love alive?

Life happens. We get caught up. With so many little details to take care of, we often forget to love each other in the small things. You might be surprised at what little effort it will take to make your husband feel special. I want to challenge you to serve him well. Offer your act of service to your husband as a service to your Lord, Jesus. You will not resent serving when you do it as unto the Lord.

Now perhaps as you are reading this, your thoughts are: *"Oh please… do I always have to be the one to make such effort? He should be thinking of me for a change! I am not going to do another nice thing for him because he doesn't deserve it! When was the last time he did something special for me?"* I can assure you, there is not a woman on the planet that hasn't thought the same thing! But, here's the deal, girlfriend…

You have two choices. You can choose to do nothing and have things remain the same, or you can choose to be pro-active and take action! In all honesty, I cannot promise you things will change overnight. I do not know the history of your relationship. But I do know these things take time. In the same way that our bodies don't go right back into place after giving birth to our children, we must allow time for situations and patterns to change when giving birth to a new way of loving our spouse.

The question is: Do you want a Godly marriage or are you willing to settle for a dead marriage? I pray you will choose a Godly marriage and take baby steps towards each other again. Surrender your heart and commit your way to Christ's power right now.

THE ELEGANT WOMAN OF GOD REALLY LISTENS, AND RESPONDS TO HER LOVED ONES ACCORDINGLY.

ELEGANT REFLECTIONS

After reading today's story entitled: *Sweet Tea with Lemons,* how were you challenged or inspired?

_____

_____

_____

_____

It is most often the simplest things that mean the most to someone—especially to our husbands. What means or (meant) the most to your man?

_____

_____

_____

_____

Do you listen to what your man wants? Are you concerned with taking care of his needs?

_____

_____

_____

_____

The spiritual order we are to follow as women of interior elegance is: 1. God, 2. Husband, 3. Children. Is your spiritual order intact?

_____

_____

_____

_____

Note: If you are a widow and you realize after reading this chapter some of the big mistakes you made, do NOT allow the enemy to defeat you. Remember, your loved one is with the Lord and He is fully satisfied. He is in the place of ALL-KNOWING and sees the big picture now. Move forward, loving the other people in your life.

When was the last time you did a random act of kindness for someone you love?

_____

_____

_____

_____

Why do we cater to the needs of certain people more removed from ourselves, while neglecting the most special people in our lives?

_____

_____

_____

_____

Note: The fact that my friend made her husband sweet tea was pretty awesome—at least to him. But the fact that she remembered how much he likes lemon in his tea, well...that kicked it up a notch! He was over-the-moon! Go the extra mile for those you love. Listen and take note of the important things—the things that speak love and respect.

Prayer: "Father, thank you for lavishing me with your love. Thank you for taking note of my needs and for going the extra mile to give me your son, Jesus. Teach me to listen and respond to those I love, accordingly." Amen.

CHAPTER FORTY-SEVEN

PUPPY CHOW

"**M**ommy, mommy, I want some skittles!" "I want M&M's!" My children screamed while tugging on my clothes, as I waited in the long line at the gas station. People began to stare as the kids whined and begged for candy, their voices growing louder and louder.

I bent down close to their faces in frustration and with a firm tone of voice said: "Hush—you guys know what I told you! There is an entire container of Puppy Chow out in the car and you will not get another snack until you have eaten it all up!"

Heads rolled my direction. Jaws dropped.

Unfortunately, they had no idea I was referring to the yummy, home-made snack-mix made of peanut butter, cereal, chocolate chips, and powdered sugar. Our family calls it: *Puppy Chow.*

All they knew was that I had scolded my children and threatened not to buy them anything to eat until they had eaten all the dog food in the container that was located out in our car.

After returning to our car, it finally dawned on me why the people in the gas station had responded with such alarm, and why they had watched our every move. No wonder the police officer had followed us out of the store—his glaring eyes escorting us all the way to the car.

As we drove away, my husband and I laughed hysterically as we replayed all that had taken place inside the gas station—the look on people's faces and the subtle police investigation we had undergone.

Many times in my life, I have been misunderstood; I have failed to remember that people's perceptions are their reality.

As a woman of interior elegance, we must make no assumptions when it comes to people and perceptions. There will be times in our lives when our sweetest offerings will be perceived as *dog food*. Although we cannot change the perceptions of others, we can control the way we string our words together.

A WOMAN OF INTERIOR ELEGANCE UNDERSTANDS THE IMPORTANCE OF GOOD COMMUNICATION, BUT KNOWS HER BEST EFFORTS WILL OFTEN BE MISUNDERSTOOD.

But I tell you that men will have to give account on the day of judgment of every careless word they have spoken. For by your words you will be acquitted, and by your words you will be condemned. Matthew 12:36 (NIV)

ELEGANT REFLECTIONS

Reread today's inspirational thought: **A woman of interior elegance understands the importance of good communication, but knows her best efforts will often be misunderstood.**

Have you ever been misunderstood? Share a funny or serious story in the space below:

_____
_____
_____
_____
_____

Why is it important to be a good communicator?

_____
_____
_____
_____
_____

A person's perception is their reality. What does this mean?

_____
_____
_____
_____
_____

How does a wrong perception affect your relationships in general? (Husband, mother, father, sister, brother, children)

_____
_____
_____
_____
_____

Reread Matthew 12:36 (NIV): *But I tell you that men will have to give account on the day of judgment of every careless word they have spoken. For by your words you will be acquitted, and by your words you will be condemned.*

Note: Women are talkers. Most of us love to talk, more than we love to eat. How many careless words do you think women speak?

_____

_____

_____

_____

_____

Read Psalm 34:8: *Oh, taste and see that the Lord is good, blessed is the man who trusts in Him.*

What do you think this means?

_____

_____

_____

_____

_____

Note: The word "taste" in Hebrew is associated with the word "good." (Hebrew Ta'am, "the sense of taste," – "perception")

Taste: To become acquainted with by experience.

(Sources: Merriam-webster.com and Bible Encyclopedia)

Note: If the people in the gas station and the police officer could have "tasted" the puppy chow, they would have known it wasn't dog food. They would have known what I was feeding my children was something delicious. Instead, all they had to go on was their perception, based on my words.

Most of our perceptions are not reality. Ask the Lord to help you discern truth in your life and relationships. Be free of wrong perceptions that create barriers between you and those you love. Over communicating is better that under communicating.

Prayer: "Father, make all of my perceptions your reality. I have tasted and seen that you are good. I want more of your wisdom in my life. Be near me. Teach me. Thank you, Father." Amen.

CHAPTER FORTY-EIGHT

SIMMERING POTPOURRI

The kettle whistled loudly. My friend, Sharon, had arrived only moments before. I was thrilled to have her in my home for tea. Our conversation was sweet. We had so much to catch up on. Before I knew it, our cups were completely empty.

"Would you like another cup of tea?" I asked.

"Oh, no thank you," Sharon said, with a smile.

"Did your tea taste ok?" I asked.

Hesitantly, she said: "It was *gooooood*—a little strong, but good."

Sharon was not a Southern girl so I knew something wasn't right when she made one syllable into four. It wasn't her nature to expand her words or exaggerate.

My eyes lowered towards her teacup. I gasped! When I read the tag hanging off the edge of her cup, all of the blood in my body felt like it ran down to my feet.

Sharon continued talking, while I had a panic-attack. To this day, I have no idea what she was talking about. Everything went completely blank.

"Sharon, are you feeling ok, honey?" I asked, sheepishly.

"I feel just fine. Why do you ask?" Sharon replied.

"Are you sure you are feeling ok?" I asked again—just to be sure she had not been mentally impaired by the concoction I had served her.

"I am fine," she said—replying inquisitively.

"Sharon, that wasn't tea! I accidentally served you a cup of apple cinnamon, simmering potpourri!"

By this time, I was nearly in tears. I tried feverishly to make a joke out of the horrible situation I was in, and teasingly said: "*Sharon, think of it this way, you will be a walking, talking, air-freshener!*" But even that didn't help to mask my embarrassment.

Ok, my elegant friends. Go ahead. Cast the first stone my way! Careful now, when you point one finger my way, you have three pointing back at you! Sure, I may have been guilty of serving my friend a cup of simmering potpourri, but how many times have you been guilty of serving your friends cups of gossip, with sugar-cubes carefully positioned to the side of your fancy, vintage teacups?

Ok! Ok! I'll admit it! I have also served my fair share of juicy gossip!

But, since I am writing a book entitled: *Becoming a Woman of Interior Elegance,* and since you picked up this book and have been reading thus far, we both should know by now that we need to hold each other to a higher standard.

Our goal, after-all, is to establish new ways of thinking. We are not the same women as we were when we began this journey together. Let's agree to carefully consider what we are serving to others each day. Instead of serving potentially toxic mixes of bitterness, anger, and resentment, let's agree to serve cups full of joy, love, and unity—and don't forget to carefully position the sugar-cube to the side of your fancy, vintage teacup!

THE ELEGANT WOMAN OF GOD SERVES TEACUPS FULL OF JOY, LOVE, AND UNITY.

He refreshes my soul. He guides me along the right paths for His name's sake.
Psalm 23:3 (NIV)

ELEGANT REFLECTIONS

Reread the inspirational thought for today: **The elegant woman of God serves teacups full of love, joy, and unity.**

Are you serving teacups full of love, joy and unity?

_____
_____
_____
_____
_____

If not, what are you serving others?

_____
_____
_____
_____
_____

Note: It would have been much easier to not tell my friend the truth about the simmering potpourri. What would have been wrong with that choice – aside from the obvious medical concerns?

_____
_____
_____
_____
_____

What have you learned from your journey thus far?

_____
_____
_____
_____
_____

Read Psalm 13:2 (NIV): How long must I wrestle with my thoughts and day after day have sorrow in my heart? How long will my enemy triumph over me?

Write your honest thoughts in the space given below.

_____

_____

_____

_____

_____

Read 2 Samuel 22:37 (NIV): *You provide a broad path for my feet, so that my ankles do not give way.*

How does this verse encourage you on your journey?

_____

_____

_____

_____

_____

Prayer: "Father, strengthen me and help me. Equip me on my journey toward spiritual maturity. Help me to stand strong, and stay on the path of becoming the woman of interior elegance. I am fully yours." Amen.

FOLLOWING the PATH

The path we originally stepped onto will continue to lead us to many other encounters that will sharpen our integrity and build godly character. We are not perfect women, but we are dedicated women, with willing hearts. We are eager to continue learning and growing as we journey on the path set before us. We will not stop striving to become women of interior elegance.

Although our feet may grow weary and the climb may seem too steep, we will not sit down on the edge of the path, or give up in defeat. Our hearts are determined.

When we do fall down, the scrapes and bruises will only serve to remind us of the strength and courage we have gained, because we did not give into defeat. Instead, we chose to stand back up!

So keep going my elegant friends, our journey is not over—even when we have turned this final page. There are many other chapters yet to be written on the pages of our lives. God is writing a beautiful story about our journey.

Share all He has done for you thus far. Many will follow in your foot-steps, as you continue to follow the path leading to *interior elegance.*

You provide a broad path for my feet, so that my ankles do not give way.—
II Samuel 22:37 (NIV)

Only be careful, and watch yourselves closely so that you do not forget the things your eyes have seen or let them slip from your heart as long as you live. Teach them to your children and to their children after them. -
Deuteronomy 4:9 (NIV)